THE WINNING MENTALITY FOR STUDENT-ATHLETES

Copyright © 2023
by Tyson Gentry
www.tysongentry.com

All rights reserved. This book or any portion thereof may not be reproduced or used in any manner whatsoever without the express written permission of the publisher except for the use of brief quotations in a book review.

24 Productions
12850 Highway 9
Suite 600-238
Alpharetta, GA 30004

ISBN: 979-8-9889453-2-1 (Paperback)
ISBN: 979-8-9889453-3-8 (eBook)

Cover design by Pix Bee Design (pixbeedesign.com)
Photo of Tyson Gentry singing Carmen Ohio copyright © Bob Gentry. All rights reserved.
Author Bio photo of Tyson Gentry copyright © by Jodi Miller, The Ohio State University. All rights reserved.

This book is available in quantity at special discount for your team, school, or group. For further information, please contact via: tysongentry.com.

First Edition September 2023
Printed in the U.S.A.

24 Productions

THE WINNING MENTALITY FOR STUDENT-ATHLETES

Strategies for Mental Toughness
in Competition and Life

TYSON GENTRY
Foreword by Jim Tressel

CONTENTS

Foreword by Jim Tressel — vii
Acknowledgments — ix

1: Mentality — 1
2: Goals — 9
3: Belief — 17
4: Strengths and Deficits — 25
5: Visualization — 35
6: Confidence — 43
7: Routine — 51
8: Self-discipline — 59
9: Distractions — 67
10: Trash Talking — 75
11: Composure — 83
12: Attitude — 91
13: What If? — 99
14: Leadership & Responsibility — 107
15: Communication — 115
16: Reloading — 123
17: Perseverance — 133
18: Mental Health — 141
19: Beyond the Game — 151

About the Author — 159

FOREWORD BY JIM TRESSEL

So often we read books penned by authors that have observed and/or studied the subject matter describing what it takes to be successful and "win." This book, *The Winning Mentality for Student-Athletes*, is written by a young man that has lived a life of winning and has traveled the journey of success in a profound way.

Tyson Gentry's football career at The Ohio State University was cut short by a career-ending spinal cord injury; however, his journey of success and his example of winning in life, has just begun.

Each and every year our OSU Football Family reviewed the key steps in our "Journey of Success." Step #1 was to dream, set goals, and create the blueprint for our journey. Step #2 was to understand and put in the work necessary to travel said journey. Step #3, the most difficult step, was to handle adversity and handle success along the way. And Finally, Step #4 was to develop the belief that would make it happen.

In my forty-eight years in Higher Education and Sport, Tyson Gentry has demonstrated the mastering of the above four steps as well or better than any young person that I have ever witnessed.

In this book, Tyson has created a tool that will have tremendous impact to every reader, young or old, athlete or scholar, that has the passion to win in their desired journey of success. He outlines eighteen key concepts to be studied. Tyson challenges the reader to learn about the concepts and to learn about themselves. Tyson sprinkles in wisdom that he has gained from others, which he has also applied to his own real-life challenging journey. At the conclusion of each chapter, Tyson provides the reader the opportunity to write their own reflections about the subject and how they plan to apply the lessons learned.

In today's highly stimulated world, there are great challenges to learn what it truly takes to win, and to fight through the enormous distractions that one faces. There is no question that there is a fierce battle for our minds, and that developing "the winning mentality" is the key to success.

Every reader will grow by digging into the wisdom of a man that has truly handled adversity and continues to demonstrate what is the winning mentality on a daily basis.

Tyson and Megan, and the entire Gentry family are an inspiration to everyone that is blessed to know them, and choose to get to know them. Dig into this masterpiece, I promise, you will be informed and inspired.

Jim Tressel

Former Head Football Coach, Youngstown State University, and The Ohio State University
President Emeritus, Youngstown State University

ACKNOWLEDGMENTS

First and foremost, I am thankful for my Lord and Savior, Jesus Christ. Despite the trials I have experienced in my lifetime, I have been blessed with more good times than bad. God has repeatedly shown me that a lot of good can come from difficult situations—as long as we maintain our faith in Him.

Secondly, I owe a huge debt of gratitude to my amazing wife, Megan. None of this would be possible without your selfless love, encouragement, and support. You are the best thing to ever happen to me and I am blessed for every day I get to have you by my side.

Third, thank you to my incredible sons, Adam and Ryan, for loving me and reminding me how much potential there is in life. I hope you learn all of the tenets contained in this book, for when life gets difficult and you question whether or not you have the will to carry on—you do!

Fourth, thank you to my parents, Bob and Gloria, for fostering my passion for sports and giving me a foundation of love, humility, and resilience. Your guidance is appreciated more than you know and I hope to provide the same love and support to Adam and Ryan.

Finally, thank you to the many teammates, coaches, and mentors I have had throughout my life. The incredible memories and the lessons I acquired over the years have gotten me through a lot of hard times and also helped bring me to where I am today. I will do my best to pay it forward and help the next generation of athletes and individuals become the best versions of themselves.

Chapter 1

MENTALITY

What separates elite athletes from good athletes? What gives them that *edge*? That *it factor*? Every day, millions of athletes spend countless hours lifting weights to get stronger and practicing their fundamentals to get better, but most of them will neglect the most important component to being exceptional.

Elite level athletes are able to block out any thoughts of doubt, focus under pressure, and operate at the highest levels when it matters the most. But how do they do it? What do they do differently? It has very little to do with how strong or fast they are. There are plenty of average athletes who are strong and fast. For the most successful competitors, it comes down to their mindset—a.k.a., their *mentality*.

The dictionary defines mentality as, "Mental power; one's mode or way of thought." Being capable of mentally adapting to different circumstances in the midst of competition, stress, and adversity will give you an advantage that most athletes would love to have. A resilient mindset will allow you to be more successful, no matter what goal(s) you are pursuing. This is what a *winning mentality* is all about.

Most people do not realize mental fortitude is something that can be learned and perfected. This book will walk you through different aspects of having a winning mentality, so you can apply it in all facets of life. There is no shortcut to success. It takes dedication, effort, patience, and resilience. However, if you can apply yourself and stay committed, you can achieve what you set your mind to.

As a former football player for The Ohio State Buckeyes, I have personally learned from people who have competed and worked at the highest levels of athletics and in the professional world. There is no single recipe for achieving greatness, but there are commonalities that will increase the likelihood of success when utilized properly and consistently.

I saw plenty of extremely athletic guys sit on the bench at Ohio State, because they did not have the mental fortitude to compete at the collegiate level. The same thing happens to a lot of guys who go on to the NFL—the mental game needed to compete at that level is even more intense. If you do not have it, you will not last. Period.

The opposite is also true: I have seen plenty of 3-star recruits and 6th round draft picks end their careers as All-Americans and Hall-of-Famers, because of their ability to compensate mentally for what they lacked physically. Their strong mentalities gave them confidence, which allowed them to compete at a higher level than they were given credit for. You can do this, too!

The things you will learn in this book are intangible—they cannot be held or instantly exchanged. In the same way that you strengthen and train your body by doing reps in the weight room, drills in practice, or laps on the track, you can fortify your mind by doing mental conditioning. It takes time, but the results speak for themselves.

The brain can be strengthened just like a muscle; it just takes a different type of repetition. Most people do not have the slightest idea how to use their mind or get the most out of it. If you do not sharpen a knife, how can you expect to get the job done efficiently or effectively? The same idea applies to your mentality.

If you have spent countless hours practicing your form and strengthening your body, what good is all of that if you mentally give up in the midst of competition? No amount of physical strength can compensate for mental weakness. If you are mentally weak, you will become dead weight that your teammates will have to carry... which is like helping your opponent win.

On the other hand, if you are more mentally resilient than your opponents, you can have your game on point while you watch them defeat themselves. Once you get in your opponent's head, you will be amazed at how easily and frequently success follows. Momentum constantly changes throughout a competition. If you can master how to avoid getting down on yourself when you make a mistake, you can swing the momentum back in your favor a lot faster.

Have you ever competed against someone who was unshakable? That competitor who never gives up? Never cracks under pressure? Tom Brady was the master at this. That is why he is the GOAT. Mental toughness is the key.

Each chapter in this book will build upon the previous chapters. Just like building a house, you need to lay a strong foundation before you can put the walls up. Then you can work on the second floor and the roof. Doing things in the right order will help the end product turn out much better. I am going to help you build a *mental fortress*.

I learned a lot over my 15 years of playing organized sports—five of which were under the instruction of Jim Tressel (winner of eight national coach of the year awards) at Ohio State. Since my athletic career came to an end, I have spent hours upon hours speaking with and learning from some of the greatest coaches and athletes in the world. I want to pay it forward and share these lessons and wisdom with the next generation of athletes.

Not only did I learn a lot about mental fortitude from playing sports, I have learned even more from being confined to a wheelchair since 2006, when I broke my neck my sophomore year at Ohio State. My time playing sports is something I often find myself thinking about and I miss it dearly. Being an athlete who can no longer play sports is like being a bird that can no longer fly. Despite this, I refuse to let my limitations hold me back. I thought I was mentally tough before my injury, but I can honestly say I have learned and grown a lot from the adversity I have been through.

I want to teach some of these things to you, in hopes that it will help you in your journey towards greatness. Your mentality is going to be the most important tool you will rely on throughout that journey. And, SPOILER ALERT: a winning mentality is going to serve you well, long after your playing days are over.

I have also included motivational quotes from other great athletes and individuals at the end of each chapter. All of these quotes were specifically chosen to go with the theme of each chapter. As a way to teach his players the importance of being successful beyond the game of football, Coach Tressel gave us all a binder of motivational quotes, stories, and messages, which he compiled throughout his coaching career. It was called *The Winner's Manual* and as a team, we would study and discuss it together every single day at the beginning of all our team meetings. I have tailored this book in a similar manner.

Once you finish each chapter, there are sections for you to write your own thoughts and notes that deal with each chapter's topic. You can read through it individually or as a team, but if you are reading as a team, be sure to discuss the concepts that stand out the most to you. Share your insights and grow together as a unit. In order to reach your goals, you need to put in the work. This book will help you along the way.

> **IMPORTANT**: None of this will work without commitment. The more you buy into these tenets, the more they will work and the more you will see results. This premise is simple, yet profound. Please never underestimate the power of belief. Otherwise, you are wasting time and effort. If you want to achieve greatness, you have to be willing to make the necessary effort and sacrifice.

WHAT OTHERS SAY ABOUT *MENTALITY*

"Sports do not build character. They reveal it." —Haywood Broun

"All our dreams can come true, if we have the courage to pursue them." —Walt Disney

"I have missed more than 9000 shots in my career. I have lost almost 300 games. 26 times I have been trusted to take the game-winning shot and missed. I failed over and over and over again in my life, and that is why I succeed."
—Michael Jordan

"Do not limit yourself. Many people limit themselves to what they think they can do. You can go as far as your mind lets you. What you believe, remember, you can achieve."
—Mary Kay Ash

"The best time to plant a tree was 20 years ago. The second best time is now." —Chinese Proverb

"I wake up every morning and think to myself, 'How far can I push this company in the next 24 hours?'" —Leah Busque

"If people are doubting how far you can go, go so far that you cannot hear them anymore." —Michael Ruiz

"We need to accept that we will not always make the right decisions; that we will screw up royally sometimes—understanding that failure is not the opposite of success, it is part of success." —Arianna Huffington

"It is no use going back to yesterday, because I was a different person then." —Lewis Carroll

"Smart people learn from everything and everyone. Average people learn from their experiences. Stupid people already have all the answers." —Socrates

"Happiness is not something ready-made. It comes from your own actions." —Dalai Lama XIV

"Your passion is waiting for your courage to catch up."
—Isabel Lafleche

"Magic is believing in yourself. If you can make that happen, you can make anything happen." —Johann Wolfgang von Goethe

"Hold the vision, trust the process." —Unknown

"Do not be afraid to give up the good to go for the great."
—John D Rockefeller

"People who wonder if the glass is half empty or half full miss the point. The glass is refillable." —Simon Sinek

"One day or day one. You decide." —Paulo Coelho

"No one is to blame for your future situation but yourself. If you want to be successful, then become successful."
—Jamin Shah

"Things may come to those who wait, but only the things left by those who hustle." —Abraham Lincoln

"Invest in your dreams. Grind now. Shine later." —Unknown

"Some people want it to happen, some people wish it to happen, others make it happen." —Michael Jordan

"Great things are done by a series of small things brought together." —Vincent van Gogh

"I did not get there by wishing for it, but by working for it."
—Estee Lauder

"Do not be pushed around by the fears in your mind. Be led by the dreams in your heart." —Roy T. Bennet

"Unsuccessful people make their decisions based on their current situation. Successful people make their decisions based on where they want to be." —Benjamin hardy

"Hustle in silence and let your success make the noise."
—Unknown

Notes

Chapter 2
GOALS

Every journey should begin with an end destination in mind, a.k.a. a *goal*. This is especially true if you are on a journey to greatness. How can you have any idea where you are headed, unless you have a destination in mind?

Your goals are what keep you motivated. Your goals are the reason you push yourself beyond your limits. The reason you push through pain. The reason you make sacrifices others are not willing to make. The reason you wake up and go, while others hit the snooze button.

You cannot expect things to just fall into place unless you have a process you follow that will result in success. This is a very simple premise, but you would be amazed at the number of people who fail because they did not think it was important enough to be organized. Do not limit your opportunities for reaching your goals, simply because you do not have a plan.

Ask any successful business owner and they will agree that you have to have a solid business plan before anything else. In order for things to line up, they need to formulate their roadmap for how they plan on making money. Achieving success in athletics is similar to business, so you have to ask yourself similar questions: what steps do you need to take to make it happen? Who can help you through the whole process? What have you seen others do in order to attain the same or similar objective? If you want to achieve greatness, you have to imitate greatness.

Another important question to ask yourself is: why do you want to achieve these goals? Are you doing it for yourself or for someone else? Is this something you are doing because you are passionate about it or because it is a means to provide a better future for yourself and others? There are many reasons, but make sure you know yours. You do not ever want to get so far down a path and then suddenly wonder why you are there. Everything you do should be intentional.

Achieving goals can be a grind and it may not always be what you envisioned once you get there. Regardless, knowing *why* you are doing something is very important to the process.

That being said, it is a good idea to keep visual reminders of your goals. Put them in places you are sure to see them throughout your day. These can be Post-It notes with inspirational messages, pictures of athletes you look up to, quotes from haters, or something that reminds you of your *why*. Use whatever it is that will fuel you and keep you motivated.

You should constantly see these reminders. Place them on the ceiling over your bed, so it is the first thing you see in the morning and the last thing you see before you close your eyes at night. Put them on your bathroom mirror, so when you see your reflection, you will have to look yourself in the eye and reaffirm your commitment. Have them in your car so you can think about them while you are stuck in traffic. The more your goals are on your mind, the faster they will manifest in reality.

Keep reminders of your goals on your phone, computer, tablets, TV, refrigerator, and anywhere else that will distract you from your mission. Chapter 9 is about distractions because achieving your goals is hard enough as it is—do not let insignificant distractions interfere with what you want to achieve.

In addition to leaving yourself visual reminders, do yourself a favor and keep a log of all your goals. It does not matter if it is on your phone or in a notebook. Write down each goal, the date, and then go back to record when you achieve them. This is a great way to keep perspective of how long and hard you had to work. It will keep you humble and help when you continue to set more goals for yourself. Plus, when you are famous, you can share this "behind the scenes" information with others!

Any accomplishment or accolade is much more gratifying if you have to work hard for it. Participation awards are for people who are not willing to put in the work to succeed. It is much better to work your butt off and come up short, than to put in half-hearted effort and be "rewarded" with some meaningless ribbon or trophy.

You can lie to yourself and convince yourself that you are "special," but you will not actually have the respect that others have earned. Trust me when I say that victory is so much sweeter when you worked your butt off to earn it. It is the journey you take to achieve your goals that ends up being the reason the payoff feels so good.

Nobody makes movies about people who have been handed everything in life. Every superhero has had to overcome some sort of trial or adversity in their past. Zero athletes have won a championship without sacrificing, playing through pain, or beating the best competition. If you want to be the best, you have to overcome the challenges and adversity to get there.

If you come up short after working hard and giving it your best shot, that disappointment should fuel you to work even harder for the next time. It is only over when you quit. The road to glory is littered with the bones of those who gave up.

Finally, you should know that you do not have to share your goals with anybody if you do not want to. Honestly, it is better to work hard in silence without worrying about the expectations of others. That way, when you achieve your goals, people will take notice and your actions will speak for themselves. This will also help eliminate putting additional pressure or stress on yourself, because you will not feel the need to accomplish things faster than necessary.

WHAT OTHERS SAY ABOUT
GOALS

"If you are bored with life, you do not get up every morning with a burning desire to do things—you do not have enough goals." —Lou Holtz

"If you do not know where you are going, you will probably end up somewhere else." —Lawrence J Peter

"Shoot for the moon. Even if you miss, you will land among the stars." —Les brown

"Set a goal and do not quit until you attain it. When you do attain it, set another goal and do not quit until you reach it. Never quit." —Bear Bryant

"The trouble with not having a goal is that you can spend your life running up and down the field and never score."
—Bill Copeland

"A goal is not always meant to be reached; it often serves simply as something to aim at." —Bruce Lee

"The great danger for most of us lies not in setting our aim too high and falling short; but in setting our aim too low, and achieving our mark." —Michelangelo

"If you aim at nothing, you will hit it every time." —Zig Ziglar

"Obstacles are those frightful things you see when you take your eyes off your goal." —Henry Ford

"You are never too old to set another goal or to dream a new dream." —C.S. Lewis

"It must be borne in mind that the tragedy of life does not lie in not reaching your goal. The tragedy lies in having no goals to reach." —Benjamin E. Mays

"People are not lazy. They simply have impotent goals—that is, goals that do not inspire them." —Tony Robbins

"Becoming a star may not be your destiny, but being the best you can be is a goal that you can set for yourself." —Brian Lindsay

"Goals are not only absolutely necessary to motivate us. They are essential to really keep us alive." —Robert H. Schuller

"The victory of success is half won when one gains the habit of setting goals and achieving them." —Og Mandino

"In life, the first thing you must do is decide what you really want. What are the costs and the results. Are the results worthy of the costs? Then make up your mind completely and go after your goal with all your might." —Alfred A. Montapart

"Setting goals is the first step in turning the invisible into the visible." —Tony Robbins

"If you want to live a happy life, tie it to a goal, not to people or things." —Albert Einstein

"The thing about goals is that living without them is a lot more fun in the short run. It seems to me, though, that the people who get things done, who lead, who grow and make an impact... Those people have goals." —Seth Godin

"In the absence of clearly defined goals, we become strangely loyal to performing trivial daily acts." —Unknown

"Goal setting is the secret to a compelling future." —Tony Robbins

"Goals are the fuel in the furnace of achievement." —Brian Tracy

"I can accept failure. Everyone fails at something. But I cannot accept not trying." —Michael Jordan

"Champions keep playing until they get it right." —Billie Jean King

"Rowing harder does not help if the boat is headed in the wrong direction." —Kenichi Ohma

"Goals are dreams with deadlines." —Unknown

"Impossible is just a word thrown around by small men who find it easier to live in the world they have been given, than to explore the power they have to change it. Impossible is not a fact. It is an opinion. Impossible is potential. Impossible is temporary. Impossible is nothing." —Muhammad Ali

"Set a goal so big that you cannot achieve it, until you grow into the kind of person who can." —Unknown

SHORT TERM GOALS
(1 YEAR OR LESS)

1. _____

2. _____

3. _____

LONG TERM GOALS
(OVER 1 YEAR)

1. _____

2. _____

3. _____

SIGNATURE   DATE

_____ _____

Notes

Chapter 3
BELIEF

It has been said that we only use 10% of our brain's actual capabilities. I think it is safe to assume we use more than that, but there is still some validity to the idea that we do not understand just how *powerful* our brains are—let alone how to use them to their full capacity.

The whole purpose of everything contained in this book is to help you be the best version of yourself—in athletics and beyond. The journey begins by knowing what your goals are and why you want to achieve those things. That is your starting point.

Now it is time to dive into the most important part: *belief* in yourself and your abilities. If you continually doubt yourself, you will continually prove yourself right. Trust me...Even if you have to *fake* having confidence in yourself, you will be a lot more successful than if you straight up doubt yourself.

First and foremost, everyone is different. You are capable of things that others are not. The opposite is also true; your abilities may not be equal to others'—but that does not mean you cannot compensate in other ways or improve on those deficits.

Secondly, even though everyone is different, it is important to remember that we all have a lot of similarities, too. This chapter is only going to skim the surface of what the human mind is capable of, but YOU are absolutely able to hone, sharpen, and improve your mental capacity. Your mind is so much more powerful than you even realize!

So, just how powerful is the human mind? To put it simply, if you truly believe something, it can become a reality. Have you ever heard of the placebo effect? Doctors and scientists see this effect when they are testing the effectiveness of new medicines.

During the trial phase of new drugs, some patients will receive the real medicine, while others are given sugar pills, which have NO medicinal properties. Yet somehow, some of the patients who receive sugar pills will show signs of improvement—because they *believed* they received the medicine that would make them better.

Have you ever heard of a false pregnancy? There have been cases where women who desperately want to become pregnant and truly *believe* they are, that their bodies will start showing signs of pregnancy—only there is no baby inside them! Their bellies will get bigger, they will start producing breastmilk, and stop having their periods—all because they believe it.

This is not as simple as believing you can fly and suddenly you will start growing wings. But the point is that our brains are so powerful, that if we truly believe it, our bodies will follow. A great quote by the famous philosopher, Confucius, says, *"The man who says 'I can' and the man who says 'I cannot,' are both correct."* Why? Because they both believe it.

My point is, if you ever hope to achieve something great, you first have to believe you can do it. This is so critical to improving your abilities in athletics, because belief translates to confidence. When you are confident in yourself, it becomes a self-fulfilling prophecy and the likelihood of success skyrockets.

When you truly believe in yourself, you will become a juggernaut. Even if you make a mistake in competition, your composure does not change, because your mind is right. These concepts are integral to having a very powerful mentality and stepping up to any opponent.

The opposite is also true: self-doubt results in a much higher probability of failure. Doubt is just as powerful as belief. If you believe you cannot achieve it—you will not. It is literally that simple.

I will end with a story that really sums up the power of belief: When I was finishing my Master's degree in rehabilitation counseling, my professor (who used to work at a prison) shared an interaction he had with an inmate who was about to be released from jail. Part of the prisoner's probation agreement was that he had to get a job, so my professor suggested doing some aptitude tests to determine his strengths and problem-solving skills.

Throughout the entire interaction and testing process, the inmate did not say much. He turned in his tests and left quietly after my professor told him they would meet to discuss everything once they were graded. The next day, they met to review the results and talk about potential employment options. The first thing my professor said to the inmate as he sat silently in his chair, was that the tests showed he had a lot of strengths and tested very highly in a number of areas.

Upon hearing this, the inmate sat up in his chair and his whole demeanor changed. He said, "I always wondered if I was more capable than people gave me credit for. All I have ever been told is that I am stupid and I will always be a nobody." Up until that point, he only doubted himself because no one else believed in him. To put it another way, the inmate believed he was a loser, so that is exactly what he became.

My professor told us the prisoner came back to visit a year or so later, to say thank you for telling him he had potential. The inmate said after he got out of jail, he separated himself from the negative people in his life who were holding him back. He also shared that he was going back to school to pursue a degree and better himself.

It is truly amazing how much your life can change if you believe in yourself! This also shows you how important it is to believe in others and give them encouragement, too. A single spark can start a giant forest fire that is capable of engulfing thousands of square miles of forest. A state, national, or world championship starts with a single idea or goal. Yes, you need to be physically capable in order to compete, but you first need to have your mind right. It all starts with belief.

WHAT OTHERS SAY ABOUT *BELIEF*

"Nobody can impose your beliefs on you. Only you can permit a belief to be true for you or not." —Marc Reclau

"Beliefs are choices. First you choose your beliefs, then your beliefs affect your choices." —Roy T. Bennett

"You are what you believe yourself to be." —Paulo Coelho

"My belief is stronger than your doubt." —Unknown

"So if you have a dream, then just believe that you can achieve it, no matter what. Even when you cannot feel deep in your heart, any words of encouragement, just believe in your dream and your heart will finally show you the way." —Shuchi Gupta

"We will need to build constructive beliefs, behavior patterns, thought patterns, habits, values and principles, to override the deconstructive ones." —Barry Naude

"A believer is never disturbed, because other people do not see the fact which he sees." —Ralph Waldo Emerson

"Great things happened to those who do not stop believing, trying, learning, and being grateful." —Roy T. Bennett

"Whatever you expect with certainty will become your very own self-fulfilling prophecy." —Bob Herring

"You can always go higher, for within yourself you are greater than you think. Believe that, for it is a fact—a great, big, truthful, wonderful fact." —Norman Vincent Peale

"Believe in the rewards that await you. Believe in the harvest in store." —Wish Belkin

"Our success is measured by personal beliefs, not by anyone else's standards or beliefs." —Henry Marsh

"Changing your negative beliefs is the first step in the transformation process that will really make a difference in your life." —Anita Foley

"Yes, beliefs are important, for they shape who we are. But our identity, is revealed not through our beliefs or our talk, but through our actions." —Thomas Ingram

"Remember that what you are is what you believe, not what you were handed genetically." —Wayne Dyer

"Whatever it is you believe about yourself, that is what others will believe about you, too." —Harvey Volson

"All beliefs and belief systems boil down to having faith in something we would like to believe to be the truth."
—Neville Berkowitz

"Myths which are believed in, tend to become true."
—George Orwell

"Be brave to stand for what you believe in, even if you stand alone." —Roy T. Bennett

"Be believing, be happy, do not get discouraged. Things will work out." —Gordon Hinckley

"My father gave me the greatest gift anyone could give another person, he believed in me." —Jim Valvano

"You may be the only person left who believes in you, but it is enough. It takes just one star to pierce a universe of darkness. Never give up." —Richelle Goodrich

"If you believe you can, you might. If you know you can, you will." —Steve Maraboli

"Believe in yourself and all that you are. Know that there is something inside you that is greater than any obstacle."
—Christian Larson

"Believe in yourself, take on your challenges, dig deep within yourself to conquer fears. Never let anyone bring you down. You have got to keep going." —Chantal Sutherland

"If you believe in yourself and have dedication and pride—and never quit, you will be a winner. The price of victory is high, but so are the rewards." —Bear Bryant

"Believe you can and you are halfway there."
—Theodore Roosevelt

"To accomplish great things, we must not only act, but also dream; not only plan, but also believe." —Anatole France

"To uncover your true potential, you must first find your own limits and then have the courage to blow past them."
—Picabo Street

"Good, better, best. Never let it rest. Until your good is better and your better is best." —Saint Jerome

3: BELIEF

I NEED TO BELIEVE THAT I CAN...

1. _____

2. _____

3. _____

4. _____

5. _____

I SHOULD NOT DOUBT THAT I CAN...

1. _____

2. _____

3. _____

4. _____

5. _____

Notes

Chapter 4

STRENGTHS AND DEFICITS

Reliability, persistence, focus, intensity, composure, energy—what do you bring to the table? In what ways can your teammates count on you? If you play an individual sport, what allows you to get out in front of your opponents?

Just reading those questions, you should have had a few things come to mind about what your mental and physical strengths are as an athlete. In a lot of ways, your mental strengths are what allow your physical strengths to truly shine. Depending on your specific strengths, you should know what scenarios or situations you thrive in.

When I used to run track, my main event was the 110m high hurdles. I have long legs and was fast, but I was not the fastest overall sprinter. The best part of my race was my start, because I worked relentlessly on my reaction time to the starting gun, as well as my drive in the first 25 meters. So, I would rely heavily on beating people out of the blocks and getting ahead early. I would then try to maintain my lead before other runners could hit their top gears and catch me. Quite often, my opponents would lose their focus and clip hurdles because they were too focused on me getting out in front so quickly. This is an example of using a strength to compensate for a deficit.

If your coach is any good at recognizing talents, he or she will know how and when to call on you to implement your strengths in the game plan. You should be prepped for every possible situation in a competition, so that the ideal person is in the right position to make the play. It is extremely important to always have a laser focused strategy/attack plan, which includes playing to your strengths.

As an athlete competing for a starting spot, you are always being evaluated by your coach, who has the job of making sure the team wins. This should be common sense, but if you do not feel you are being utilized properly, ask your coach if you can sit down to talk it over. Communication between players and coaches is crucial, and we will cover it in more detail later.

What about your deficits? What are they? Have you given up and accepted them? It may seem counterintuitive, but one of your strengths should be knowing what your deficits are. If you acknowledge them, it will allow you to work on them and strengthen them to get better.

I want to specifically point out that I did not use the word "weaknesses." This is because weakness implies that you are weak—which I know is not the case. Every competitor has a deficit, which simply means they have aspects to their game that they would like to make better. Whatever your deficits are, do not accept or neglect them!

Even the best athletes in the world have deficits they would like to improve upon. Through repetition and focus, they zero in on these parts of their game and annihilate them. You can do the same; it just takes a lot of dedication and hard work.

Additionally, knowing your deficits will help you determine when and how you should rely on your teammates. There are many different scenarios I could use, but if you are not the right person for a specific play, event, or strategy, then help identify the teammate who is.

Acknowledging your teammates' strengths will help you elevate your status as a selfless leader, as well as boost their confidence because of your belief in them. All great leaders understand how to capitalize on the advantages they have and work around any disadvantages.

4: STRENGTHS AND DEFICITS

Ultimately, this understanding will make you a better competitor and teammate.

Strengths and deficits do not always have to be skill related, either. Are you more suited to be the team leader, whom everyone looks to when the game is on the line? Some people crave that because it is who they are. They do not mind the pressure and thrive when it is time to step up. If you are this type of competitor, great! Every team needs someone who can throw everyone on their back and carry them to victory.

This role can come with some pitfalls, though. If you want to be the one to take the game-winning shot and you miss, you will be the one who has to deal with that burden—the guilt of letting your team down, negative headlines, and of course, angry fans. If you want to bask in the sunshine of glory, you have to be willing to deal with the storm clouds of grief, too. *"Heavy is the head that wears the crown,"* as they say.

Otherwise, are you more suited for a second-in-command or supporting role? You may not always get your picture in the paper, but you are just as important to the team. The general may be the one calling the shots, but he or she cannot be effective without colonels, majors, and soldiers to carry out the orders.

Also, if you are not a team captain, there is less pressure on you, which you might prefer. There is nothing wrong with not wanting the responsibilities or stress that comes with being the one in charge. However, the team leader cannot do everything alone, so that could be a perfect role for you—to be the one he or she looks for when in trouble. On a team, everybody has a job and all of them are important.

If you do not play a team sport, there is really no way to hide your deficits. You can only rely on yourself and your coach to utilize your strengths in the game plan. From there, you will have to make adjustments when needed. This means you need to be able to adapt and recover quickly.

The other side of preparing for competition is knowing your opponent's strengths and deficits. This can be accomplished by studying film and dissecting things so you can complete your game plan. How will you exploit their deficits? You cannot win if you do not score, so taking advantage of the cracks in their game is very important.

Alternatively, how will you handle your opponent's strengths? By strategizing and knowing how to shut down their main plan of attack, you can get them frustrated and off their game. Sometimes, the best offense is a good defense—they cannot win if you do not let them score. Knowing these things will help in the execution of your game plan.

Regardless of how long you have been competing or how good you think you are, you should always be working to hone your skills. Athletes and the sports they play are always evolving. Keep building up your arsenal, so no one stands a chance when they step on the playing field against you. You need to get to the point where you become a force to be reckoned with. Even if you have a couple slight deficits, your competition cannot even begin to handle all of your strengths!

WHAT OTHERS SAY ABOUT *STRENGTHS & DEFICITS*

"Talent wins games, but teamwork and intelligence wins championships." —Michael Jordan

"Every weakness contains within itself, a strength."
—Shusaku Endo

"If you cannot fly, then run. If you cannot run, then walk. If you cannot walk, then crawl. Whatever you do, you have to keep moving forward." —Martin Luther King Jr.

"To acknowledge your weakness is to understand your vulnerability; to understand your vulnerability is to know your strength." —Criss Jami

"A brave man acknowledges the strength of others."
—Veronica Roth

"We are stronger, tougher, braver more resilient, than any of us imagine." —Mark Nepo

"My attitude is that if you push me towards something that you think is a weakness, then I will turn that perceived weakness into a strength." —Michael Jordan

"A fear of weakness only strengthens the weakness." —Criss Jami

"All of us are talented in our unique way. We just need to recognize our capacity and develop our talents to their full potential." —Unknown

"We do not even know how strong we are until we are forced to bring that hidden strength forward." —Isabell Allende

"Life is very interesting... In the end, some of your greatest pains become your greatest strengths." —Drew Barrymore

"Giants are not what we think they are. The same qualities that appear to give them strength are often the source of a great weakness." —Malcolm Gladwell

"Where there is no struggle, there is no strength."
—Oprah Winfrey

"Great occasions do not make heroes or cowards; they simply unveil them to the eyes of men. Silently and perceptibly, as we wake or sleep, we grow strong or weak; at last some crisis shows what we have become." —Brooke Foss Wescott

"Weak people believe what is forced on them. Strong people believe what they wish to believe, forcing that to be real."
—Gene Wolfe

"Real talent shines through, regardless of how many others there are around you." —Paloma Faith

"It is the destiny of the weak to be devoured by the strong."
—Otto von Bismarck

"True happiness involves the full use of one's power and talents." —John W. Gardner

"Talent is a universal gift, but it takes a lot of courage to use it. Do not be afraid to be the best" —Paulo Coelho

"Talent is truth on display." —Teri Rossio

"Strategy will compensate the talent. The talent will never compensate the strategy." —Marco Pierre White

"Embrace your talent and pursue it. You will not believe what you can accomplish." —Unknown

"If you have talent, use it in every which way possible. Do not hoard it. Do not dole it out like a miser. Spend it lavishly, like a millionaire intent on going broke." —Brenda Francis

"With the right mindset, you can turn your weaknesses into your strengths." —Benjamin Berg

"Know what your strengths are, but also keep in mind what your weaknesses are; always work on your weaknesses."
—Cain Velasquez

"Sometimes we are tested, not to show our weaknesses, but to discover our strengths." —Unknown

MY STRENGTHS ARE:

1. _____

2. _____

3. _____

4. _____

5. _____

MY DEFICITS ARE:

1. _____

2. _____

3. _____

4. _____

5. _____

4: STRENGTHS AND DEFICITS

Notes

Chapter 5

VISUALIZATION

Have you ever pictured yourself hitting the game-winning shot at the buzzer? What about making a great defensive stop to win the game? Maybe you have thought about what it would be like to come back from a big deficit in a race?

All of these are basic examples of *visualization*. Elite level athletes use a more in-depth form of visualization as a training tool because it helps them hone their concentration and technique. You can do it, too.

If your goal is a seed, belief is the water it needs to grow into something tangible. Water that seed enough and you will reap the rewards. Visualization is the perfect mental training tool to enhance your belief.

I am sure you have heard the phrase, *"Seeing is believing."* Visualization is simply seeing something in your *mind's eye*. When you can see it clearly in your head, you are more likely to believe you can do it. Before you even step on the playing field, you should visualize yourself performing flawlessly. When the mind believes, the body follows, right?

If you visualize what you desire in great detail, you will increase your chances of eventually manifesting it into reality. The key is to focus and visualize those details—the more, the better. What are your surroundings? What scenario are you in? Are you going against an opponent or just visualizing what you need to do? What specific part of your game are you visualizing? You are in total control of what you see in your mind, so make it ideal. Tune everything else out—the only thing you should hear is your thoughts.

Even if you picture something that seems impossible or above your skill level, visualization can help get you there. Coax your subconscious into believing IT IS POSSIBLE. Reprogram your mind to have more confidence, a faster reaction time, flawless execution, and total control over every aspect of your game.

If you can master visualization, you will be able to enhance the muscle memory you develop in practice. Pairing muscle memory with mental reinforcement will help your instincts to take over in the heat of battle. It is another weapon in your arsenal. Mental reps are just as crucial as reps in the weight room or on the practice field.

It does not matter what sport you play. Each one has unique aspects that can be precisely analyzed and fine-tuned. It also does not matter what position you play. Each one requires specific techniques that can be perfected. Visualization can help with all of this.

If you do it enough, you will consistently get the results you practiced mentally. Obviously, you cannot just lay around thinking about what you need to do and suddenly you get better at it. Visualization should be used to supplement actual practice, but the more clearly you can picture what you need to do, the more effective it is.

Visualization can also be used to help you work through difficult situations that might happen in athletics. If you want to be fully prepared, you need to be able to adapt and recover when faced with adversity in competition and in life. These are called contingencies.

What if you make a mistake at a crucial point in a game? What if the crowd will not stop taunting you? What if you get injured? What if your opponent does a lot of trash talking? Do you ever think about these things? If you do not, you should.

We will cover other "what if" scenarios in more detail in a later chapter. This is because it is important to not only prepare for positive outcomes, but also for when things do not go your way. There is an old adage that says, *"Luck favors the prepared."* If you really want to be mentally prepared for any and all outcomes, visualization is one way to ensure you will be more prepared than your opponents.

Like I mentioned in the Belief chapter, your brain is a powerful weapon. Getting it dialed in by sharpening your mental acuity is the key to maintaining your concentration, composure, and confidence while you are competing. Visualization is a tool you can use to enhance all of these things. With practice, you can master this technique and take your game to a whole new level.

PRO TIPS FOR UTILIZING *VISUALIZATION*

1. Select a comfortable and quiet room, preferably where you can lay down. You do not want anyone or anything to interrupt you.
2. Start by clearing your mind of all extraneous thoughts or worries. Put ALL distractions out of your mind.
3. Think about relaxing your entire body, starting with your toes and slowly working all the way up to the tip of your head (this should take 2-3 minutes). Try to maintain this throughout the visualization process.
4. Think about whatever part of your game you are trying to improve or reinforce, and break it down into individual parts. What specifically needs improved? How would you like to do it every time in competition? The more detailed your thoughts, the better. Focus on one component at a time—do not jump around.
5. Visualize exactly what it should look like when you actually do it. Like watching game film, you have the ability to go backwards and forwards in your mind, watching yourself perform flawlessly.
6. Make sure you are thinking positive thoughts and reinforcing the fact that you CAN and WILL perform exactly the way you want to. Remember, the person who says *"I can"* and the person who says *"I cannot,"* are both correct.
7. Repeat this process weekly.

WHAT OTHERS SAY ABOUT *VISUALIZATION*

"You must feed your mind, even as you feed your body—and to make your mind healthy, you must feed it good, nourishing, wholesome thoughts." —Norman Vincent Peale

"I like visualizing a lot, so the night before a competition and right before, I will visualize myself. I will close my eyes, turn away from everybody, and just see myself doing exactly what I want to accomplish." —Kacy Catanzaro

"We are told that talent creates opportunity, yet it is desire that creates talent." —Bruce Lee

"No one whoever gave their best, regretted it." —George Halas

"If you are not going all the way, why go at all?" —Joe Namath

"The secret of all those who make discoveries, is that they regard nothing as impossible." —Justice Liebig

"Visualize the thing you want. See it, feel it, believe in it. Make your mental blueprint and begin to build." —Robert Collier

"I visualize things in my mind before I have to do that. It is like having a mental workshop." —Jack Youngblood

5: VISUALIZATION

"I think in order to accomplish anything in life, you have to visualize yourself there—accepting the award, hearing your song on the radio, whatever it is—or you will lose the willpower and the drive." —Daya

"When I meditate, I visualize myself after the match as a winner." —Bianca Andreescu

"It does not always work out, but if I visualize myself getting what I want, it is more likely to happen." —Stella Maxwell

"Any professional athlete will tell you that the mind is everything. For me, there is no shame in saying that I use visualization, because it really works." —Carli Lloyd

"You visualize making a game changing play. That is what you are here for." —Aaron Donald

"You can visualize and you can trick yourself into thinking a certain way. There is all kinds of things you can do to try to get into the right spot mentally." —Kyle Korver

"First you visualize, then you materialize." —Denis Waitley

"Practice makes progress, not perfect." —Unknown

"Losers visualize the penalties of failure. Winners visualize the rewards of success." —William S. Gilbert

"I believe that visualization is one of the most powerful means of achieving personal goals." —Harvey Mackay

"Visualization. It may be the most important part of your mental package. "—Ray Floyd

"The mind will not believe what it cannot see." —Unknown

"Stop being afraid of what could go wrong and start being excited about what could go right." —Tony Robbins

"To accomplish great things, we must first dream, then visualize, then plan... Believe... Act!" —Alfred A. Montapert

"Dare to visualize a world in which your most treasured dreams come true." —Ralph Marston

"The harder you work and visualize something, the luckier you get." —Seal

"Visualization is daydreaming with a purpose." —Bo Bennett

"Proper visualization by the exercise of concentration and willpower enables us to materialize thoughts, not only as dreams or visions in the mental realm, but also as experiences in the material realm." —Paramahansa Yogananda

"The key to effective visualization is to create the most detailed, clear and vivid picture to focus on."
—George St. Pierre.

I CAN IMPROVE MY _____ WITH VISUALIZATION:

1. _____

2. _____

3. _____

4. _____

5. _____

MY (ANSWERS FROM ABOVE) CAN BE BROKEN DOWN INTO THESE INDIVIDUAL COMPONENTS:

1. _____

2. _____

3. _____

4. _____

5. _____

Notes

Chapter 6
CONFIDENCE

Now that you know a little more about how powerful your mind is, and also realizing you can increase your mental capacity with mental exercises, you begin to understand just how much potential you really have. Believing in yourself and your capabilities translates to one thing: *confidence*.

If you are confident in yourself, your performance on the field of play will be consistently better. This increases your likelihood of winning and accomplishing your goals. Building your confidence is like building a house out of bricks...It is done one piece at a time.

Imagine having most of the pieces to a puzzle. You can put them together and be content with knowing what most of the picture is, but you do not actually have the complete package. Do you want to be content or do you want to be confident? The answer is obvious.

If you look around at your competition, how many of them seem to be physically capable but do not have the mentality that truly sets them apart from everyone else? All those muscles do not mean a thing if you are not mentally strong. It is like having a really fast car with a student driver behind the wheel. Horsepower is useless if you do not know how to drive.

On the opposite side, have you ever gone up against an opponent who did not look like he or she would be much of a threat—but they ended up being a lot more talented than you thought? It is amazing how being mentally stout and having confidence in yourself can compensate for a deficit of physical prowess.

I want to get you to a point where you believe in yourself AND you have all the pieces to the puzzle. So as soon as you step on the playing field, you have confidence you are going to execute flawlessly. Your opponents will mentally implode when they realize they stand no chance against you.

I am not going to lie, it is an incredible thing to watch your opponent mentally give up. I bet you know what I am talking about—you can see it all over their face. They give up because there are no cracks in your game and they know it is useless to even try. When it happens, you can literally have your way with them. This is just the beginning of mental warfare.

As a quick side-note, do not forget that the opposite is also true: you should never let your opponent see that your confidence is broken. We will discuss composure later on, but since it goes hand-in-hand with confidence, it needs to be said here as well.

If your opponent knows you are starting to doubt yourself or question whether or not you are good enough, it is like blood in the water with sharks. Do not ever give them the satisfaction. If you give your best effort and do not give up, you can still hold your head high if you lose. Your competition should always challenge you—otherwise you are not competing against the right people. Play your hardest until the clock says 00:00 or the competition ends.

Confidence is something you should have a lot of, but at the same time, you do not want to be overconfident. The first reason you do not want too much confidence is because you could let your guard down, causing you to overlook critical details. This could lead to your downfall.

Have you ever missed a layup, dropped a ball that was right in your hands, or missed a gimme putt? It is such an easy play that you lose focus and you end up making a critical mistake. Being overly confident can leave you feeling overly stupid.

What about losing to an unworthy competitor? There are far too many instances where a lesser opponent beat a person or team that should win 100 out of 100 matchups. On any given day, even the best competitor has the potential to lose. Do not learn this lesson the hard way. I have never heard someone say they were too focused on the fundamentals. Please believe me when I tell you that these types of losses will haunt you for a long time.

A second reason you should not have too much confidence is because there is a fine line between confidence and arrogance. If you are the best, people are going to put a bullseye on your back and gun for you. But if you are cocky and arrogant, they are going to put a bullseye on your back and fire missiles at you.

They will make it their sole purpose to bring you down and revel in your defeat. Do not give them the ammunition they need to make that happen. (As another side-note, some people enjoy having a bullseye on their back. If that is you, I will go over strategies at a later point).

A third reason too much confidence is a bad thing is because, in addition to your opponents wanting your head on a chopping block, your teammates or coach(es) could quickly grow to resent you. Your overconfidence can easily come across as arrogance and this could fracture a team's chemistry. If this happens, fixing it can be really difficult—especially if you do not like apologizing.

Your confidence should be contagious. You want to have enough confidence that your team will feed off of it and it will raise their level of play. They will look to you in clutch moments and know that you can lead them to victory when called upon. It is magical when this happens.

My point is, you can be confident and humble at the same time. Being humble, yet confident is a great way to win and still have the respect of your teammates and opponents. Just so you know, if you are the best at something—no matter what you do—there will always be haters. However, winning with class is the best way to be on top.

Ultimately, confidence is directly linked to belief. At this point, you know that if you believe it, you can achieve it. Confidence is the manifestation of belief. As long as you do not doubt yourself, you will continue to make gains and improve as an athlete and person.

WHAT OTHERS SAY ABOUT *CONFIDENCE*

"Too much ego will kill your talent." —Unknown

"When you have a lot of confidence and you feel like nobody can beat you, it is game over for everyone else." —Jason Day

"As is our confidence, so is our capacity." —William Hazlitt

"Confidence is contagious. So is a lack of confidence."
—Vince Lombardi

"When you have confidence, you can do anything."
—Sloane Stephens

"All you need in this life is ignorance and confidence, and then success is sure." —Mark Twain

"Confidence is a line of this game or any game. If you do not think you can win, you will not." —Jerry West

"Confidence comes from hours and days and weeks and years of constant work and dedication." —Roger Staubach

"The most incredible thing you can wear is confidence."
—Unknown

"Confidence is a very fragile thing." —Joe Montana

"Confidence comes from discipline and training."
—Robert Kitosaki

"When you have confidence, you can have a lot of fun. And when you have fun, you can do amazing things." —Joe Namath

"Experience tells you what to do; confidence allows you to do it." —Stan Smith

"Confidence if you have it, you can make anything look good."
—Diane von Furstenberg

"Inhale confidence, exhale doubt." —Unknown

"With confidence, you have won before you have started."
—Marcus Garvey

"If you do not have any confidence, you are not going to do anything." —Stefon Diggs

"The circulation of confidence is better than the circulation of money." —James Madison

"Confidence is the most important single factor in this game, and no matter how great your natural talent, there is only one way to obtain and sustain it: Work." —Jack Nicklaus

"For if you train hard and responsibly, your confidence surges to a maximum." —Floyd Patterson

"Successful people often exude confidence—it is obvious that they believe in themselves and what they are doing. Their success may make them more confident, but their confidence was there first." —Travis Bradberry

"Sometimes, if you fake confidence long enough, you are going to be confident." —Elle King

"For me, it is always been about preparation. The more prepared I can be each week, the less pressure I feel and the more confident I am. As your confidence grows, it is only natural that the pressure you feel diminishes."
—Aaron Rodgers

"Self-confidence is a superpower. Once you start to believe in yourself, magic starts happening." —Unknown

"Doubt kills more dreams than failure ever will."
—Suzy Kassem

"I am building a fire, and every day I train, I add more fuel. At just the right moment, I light the match." —Mia Hamm

"When you have got something to prove, there is nothing greater than a challenge." —Terry Bradshaw

"Everything you want is on the other side of fear."
—Jack Canfield

I WOULD LIKE TO IMPROVE MY CONFIDENCE IN:

1. _____

2. _____

3. _____

4. _____

5. _____

I SHOULD NOT BE OVERCONFIDENT WHEN I:

1. _____

2. _____

3. _____

4. _____

5. _____

Notes

Chapter 7
ROUTINE

It is impossible to be the best at anything if you are not consistent. Coca-Cola is one of the most recognizable brands and has been loved by billions of people for close to 150 years...but how? Why? Because they made consistency a top priority. It would not be Coca-Cola if the flavor changed every time you open a new can. Companies use quality control to make sure their products are all consistently the same over time.

So how do you get consistent results in athletics? *Routine.* Top tier competitors make sure they keep the same routines so they will get consistent results when going from practice to competition. It does not make any sense to practice/prepare differently than how you will perform when you step onto the playing field.

I know the concept of "practice makes perfect" has been drilled in to you over and over again. There is a reason for this. It is amazing what people have been able to train themselves to do—*perfectly*—simply because they have done it thousands of times. Musicians are a great example of this. If you want to be great and you care enough, you need to establish a routine.

Starting with your warm-up, you should be sure to get your mind and body prepared and ready to go full speed. Visualize, meditate, pray, stretch, do calisthenics, listen to music, etc. Find what works well for you and stick with it. The minute you start to neglect this routine, you will open yourself up to inconsistency and injury. Not only is this crucial for allowing you to practice full speed (just like you will play in competition), it is going to help you compete for a long time because you are taking care of your mind and body.

The best athletes have great reflexes and instincts. There is no arguing this. How did they hone these skills? By doing it over and over until it became second nature. By the time they step on the playing field, these skills are well established and instincts take over without even needing to think about it. Do not forget though, their focus is always locked in.

Your coaches run practice and tell you what drills to do, but that does not mean you cannot take time afterwards to do some fundamental drills on your own. Catch 100 passes, sink 100 putts, set 100 balls, make 100 free throws, and anything else you would like to be able to do confidently when everything is on the line. Tell yourself practice is not over until you do these things. The best competitors make it a routine to go above and beyond.

After practice is done, you need to have a recovery routine. Cool down, stretch, cold tub, visit the training room, replenish fluids/nutrients, proper rest/sleep, and whatever else you have to do to get your mind and body back to where they need to be. That way, you can do it all over again with minimal aches, pains, or mistakes. You have to do this every time you exert yourself. If you do not recover, you will fall behind and again, open yourself up to injuries.

This book is going to help you get your mind right so you can use your body to its fullest potential. With that in mind, having a workout routine is crucial to making sure your body is in peak condition. Lifting weights, doing plyometrics/resistance training, and cardio conditioning all need to be part of your workout routine. No one just shows up on game day and wins without putting in work behind the scenes.

Working out and conditioning should be done at least three times a week, if not more. This is not optional, either. It may not be fun, but it is completely necessary if you want to achieve any legitimate goals. Keep a workout journal and track how you have strengthened, improved, and disciplined your body to get better over time. Reflect on it for motivation to keep pushing yourself.

Additionally, diet routine is an extremely important aspect to performing at your best. For some reason, a lot of athletes neglect their nutrition. Your body is your instrument—it should always be kept in tune. If you put diesel fuel in a regular engine, do you think it will run properly? The same goes for the food you put into your body. Make sure it is part of your routine to have a healthy, balanced diet so you can perform to the best of your abilities.

Routine is very similar to habit. We can have good habits and bad habits. When you do something repetitively, it becomes ingrained and you eventually do it without even thinking or realizing. I want you to develop a consistent routine for preparation, so you will develop a habit of consistency. You become the habits you keep.

Procrastination and cheating are the enemies of routine. If you allow yourself to put things off or you neglect the crucial elements to perfecting your craft, that will become your new routine and habit. This cannot happen!

You may think to yourself, *"I have got plenty of time, I do not need to do it right now."* Before you know it, something else needs your time and attention, and the day is gone. Or maybe you cut corners on your diet, workout, or recovery, resulting in your body suffering because of it. Do what needs to be done when it needs to get done—even on the days that you do not feel like doing it!

Your routine needs to be the same every time. From the way you sleep, eat, warm up, practice, train, recover, and everything in between. It can always be tweaked and improved upon, like when you learn a new technique or a better way of doing something. But, once you figure out the correct techniques (ingredients), you need to make sure you remember your process (recipe), so your end result is victory (perfect product). This is all routine.

WHAT OTHERS SAY ABOUT *ROUTINE*

"Hard work beats talent, when talent does not work." —Tim Notke

"If you cannot outplay them, outwork them." —Ben Hogan

"You cannot get much done in life if you only work on the days when you feel good." —Jerry West

"Whether or not you reach your goals in life depends entirely on how well you prepare for them and how badly you want them." —Ronald McNair

"I believe that if you put in the work, the results will come. I do not do things half-heartedly. Because if I do, I can expect half-hearted results." —Michael Jordan

"The hallmark of success and the test of greatness, is consistency." —Unknown

"Where are you spend your attention is where you spend your life." —James Clear

"I do not care what you are trying to accomplish, you cannot skip fundamentals if you want to be the best. The moment you get away from fundamentals—whether it is proper technique, work ethic, or mental preparation—the bottom will fall out of whatever you are doing." —Michael Jordan

"We are what we repeatedly do. Excellence then, is not an act, but a habit." —Aristotle

"You have got to get up every morning with determination if you are going to go to bed with satisfaction." —George Lorimer

"Never stop doing your best just because someone does not give you credit." —Kamari aka Lyrikal

"If you work on something a little bit every day, you end up with something that is massive." —Kenneth Goldsmith

"Nothing will work unless you do." —Maya Angelou

"Do not tell everyone your plans. Instead, let them see your results." —Unknown

"Successful people are not gifted; they just work hard, then succeed on purpose." —G.K. Nelson

"Do not watch the clock. Do what it does and keep going."
—Sam Levinson

"It is not what you do once in a while, it is what you do day in and day out that makes the difference." —Jenny Craig

"Success is not always about greatness. It is about consistency. Consistent hard work leads to success. Greatness will come."
—Dwayne Johnson

"If you have good habits, time becomes your ally. All you need is patience." —James Clear

"Every day do something that will inch you closer to a better tomorrow." —Doug Firebaugh

"A lot can happen in a year. Whatever seems almost impossible today can be your new reality soon. Stay consistent and give 100%." —Gal Shapira

"Do something today that your future self will thank you for."
—Unknown

"Long-term success is a direct result of what you achieve every day. Goals provide your daily routine." —Rick Pitino

"Look for magic in the daily routine." —Lou Barlow

"Your ability to discipline yourself, to set clear goals, and then to work towards them every day, will do more to guarantee your success than any other single factor." —Brian Tracy

"The secret of your future can be found in your daily routine."
—Mike Murdoc

"You'll never change your life until you change something you do daily. The secret to your success is found in your daily routine." —John C. Maxwell

"Master your daily routine so you can master your success."
—Unknown

"Routine will take you farther than willpower."
—Shane Parrish

I HAVE ESTABLISHED ROUTINES FOR:

1. _____

2. _____

3. _____

4. _____

5. _____

MY ROUTINES CAN BE IMPROVED IN THE FOLLOWING AREAS:

1. _____

2. _____

3. _____

4. _____

5. _____

Notes

Chapter 8

SELF-DISCIPLINE

Once you have your routines established, you have to maintain them. Routines are created with consistency, but they are maintained with *self-discipline*. Unless you have a manager or a personal assistant, it is up to you to ensure you do not slack off in your responsibilities.

You would not be reading this book if you did not want to be a winner. Well, winners have self-discipline and losers do not. People who allow themselves to take the day off, skip lifting, eat junk food, slack off, or simply give up—all lack self-discipline. You either want to be a winner or you do not.

We tend to associate discipline with punishment, but I want you to think of it more as correction. When a parent disciplines their child, they are trying to correct a bad behavior. They are trying to teach lessons and the overall goal is for the child to learn right from wrong.

Basically, I want you to think of self-discipline as having self-control. People who lack self-control are easily swept away by distractions (which is covered in the next chapter). Instead of getting up early, working out, and taking nutrition seriously, they would rather lay around, play video games, and eat unhealthy food. You need to have the self-discipline to say "NO" to temptation and laziness, and then have the self-control to listen.

What is the point in setting goals if you are not committed to seeing them through? Show me a person who halfheartedly sets goals and I will show you someone who is going to be accustomed to failure and mediocrity throughout life. Self-discipline separates those who achieve their goals, from those who always have an excuse for why they are not successful.

Do not look back and live with regret because you were not willing to have some self-discipline. Yes, getting up early to work out can be rough. Having to go to school all day and then stay afterwards to go to practice is not the most fun thing in the world. Eating right and sticking to a diet is not nearly as enjoyable as eating greasy food and candy.

Working your butt off to achieve your goals takes sacrifice. You have to have the willpower and self-discipline to take the path less traveled. Most people avoid this path because it is overgrown with weeds, has a lot of twists and turns, and it is a long, slow journey. However, when you make it to the end, you get to enjoy all the fruits of your labor.

The highway to mediocrity is filled with tons of people, because most would rather take the easy route. Having self-discipline is one of the most difficult things to do if you want to be great. There is no easy route to greatness! Anything worth attaining in life has to be earned. Real winners are willing to pay that price.

You have to discipline your body to be stronger and more resilient through practice, training, lifting weights, diet, etc. Before you *physically* do any of that, you have to *mentally* make up your mind and do it! If an instrument is not tuned correctly, it sounds terrible. Are you disciplined enough to keep your instrument in tune?

Self-discipline is not only important in preparation, it is extremely important in execution. When your coach tells you the game plan and what your assignments are, you need to follow through with your responsibilities. If everyone else on your team is doing their job, but you decide to do what you think is best, mistakes are made.

Football is a perfect example of this. With 11 guys on the field, everyone needs to do their assignment for the play to work. If only 10 of them do their jobs correctly, the play will not go as planned and the other team gets the upper hand. My football coaches used to hound us on this when we would watch film as a team.

This applies to individual sports, too. If you practice a certain way and come up with a specific game plan, your coach is going to expect you to execute everything that way on game day. Do not call an audible and throw all your hard work and preparation out the window.

It is not fun getting called out for a lack of discipline. It is always better to *have discipline* in competition, than to *get disciplined* later. Study your playbook, make sure you understand your responsibilities, and be disciplined to do your job.

Those who can master themselves, can more readily master the things others only dream about. If you are serious about your goals and accomplishing great things, you need to be serious about controlling your mind. Self-discipline is an internal battle of your will.

Willpower is the life force of self-discipline. Why are so many people overweight, lazy, jobless, and unhappy? The majority of it boils down to a lack of willpower and self-discipline. Just about every excuse that most of these people can come up with can be traced back to these two sources.

People do not realize they have a lot more control over the outcomes of these things. The irony of it all, is that they are not willing to put in the work because it is *difficult*—yet, being overweight, jobless, and unhappy seems like it would be a lot more difficult than being healthy, holding down a job, and pursuing things that make them happy. Sometimes, the grass *seems* greener, but it actually is not.

You can have coaches, trainers, mentors, and plenty of other people to tell you *exactly* what you need to do to succeed, but it is all pointless if YOU do not have self-discipline to follow through on their instructions.

It all starts with having the right mentality. The body will do what the mind determines. Train your mind to immediately banish any thoughts of doubt, laziness, or anything else that will leave you short of your goals.

WHAT OTHERS SAY ABOUT *SELF-DISCIPLINE*

"You have power over your mind—not outside events. Realize this and you will find strength." —Marcus Aurelius

"Mastering others is strength, mastering yourself is true power."
—Lao Tzu

"It is not the mountain we conquer, but ourselves."
—Edmund Hillary

"There is no such thing as a great talent, without great willpower." —Honore de Bazac

"Without self-discipline, success is impossible, period." —Lou Holtz

"From sports, the greatest thing I have learned is discipline achieves goals." —Desmond Green

"It is about discipline. It is about following instructions. It is about the execution of the plan. That is what sports are."
—Ian Miller

"It is character that got us out of bed, commitment that moved us into action, and discipline that enabled us to follow through." —Zig Ziglar

"I hated every minute of training, but I said, 'Do not quit. Suffer now and live the rest of your life as a champion.'"
—Muhammad Ali

8: SELF-DISCIPLINE

"You can either experience the pain of discipline or the pain of regret. The choice is yours." —Unknown

"The hard days are what make you stronger." —Aly Raisman

"Opportunity is missed by most people because it is dressed in overalls and looks like work." —Thomas Edison

"Go the extra mile. It is never crowded there." —Dr. Wayne D Dyer

"Success is no accident. It is hard work, perseverance, learning, studying, sacrifice, and most of all, love of what you are doing or learning to do." —Pele

"A surplus of effort could overcome a deficit of confidence."
—Sonia Sotomayer

"No one has ever made a difference by being like everyone else." —The Greatest Showman

"There may be people that have more talent than you, but there is no excuse for anyone to work harder than you."
—Derek Jeter

"I never dreamt of success. I worked for it." —Estee Lauder

"A goal is a dream with a deadline." —Napoleon Hill

"With self-discipline, most anything is possible."
—Theodore Roosevelt

"Respect your efforts, respect yourself. Self-respect leads to self-discipline. When you have both firmly under your belt, that is real power." —Clint Eastwood

"Happiness is dependent on self-discipline. We are the biggest obstacles to our own happiness. It is much easier to do battle with society and with others than to fight our own nature."
—Dennis Prager

"We all have dreams. But in order to make dreams come into reality, it takes an awful lot of determination, dedication, effort, and self-discipline." —Jesse Owens

"In reading the lives of great people, I found that the first victory they won was over themselves... Self-discipline with all of them came first." —Harry S. Truman

"By constant self-discipline and self-control, you can develop greatness of character." —Grenville Kleiser

"Self-discipline is an act of cultivation. It requires you to connect today's actions to tomorrow's results. There is a season for sewing and a season for reaping. Self-discipline helps you know which is which." —Gary Ryan Blair

"The only discipline that lasts is self-discipline."
—Bum Phillips

"I think self-discipline is something like a muscle. The more you exercise it, the stronger it gets." —Daniel Goldstein

I FIND IT HARDEST TO PRACTICE SELF-DISCIPLINE WITH:

1.
2.
3.
4.
5.

PEOPLE WHO LACK SELF-DISCIPLINE WILL:

1.
2.
3.
4.
5.

Notes

Chapter 9
DISTRACTIONS

Now that you know just how important self-discipline is, it is time to dive into the things that will test your resolve. When we first got started, I had you write down your goals. I also had you sign your name to show that you are giving your word that you will put in the work and not let things come in between you and achieving those goals.

If you want people to recognize and respect your name when they hear it, you need to take your commitments seriously. Are people going to associate your name with integrity, hard work, and focus? Or, will words like lazy, uncommitted, and distractible come to mind?

Losers have things they want, but will not do what it takes to earn them. *Winners* know they have to make sacrifices to achieve greatness. Losers have *wishes*. Winners have *goals*. What separates the two? *Distractions*.

Are you willing to make the necessary sacrifices and cut out or limit any distractions that are keeping you from achieving your goals? Social media, video games, TV, girlfriends/boyfriends, parties, drinking/illegal drugs, etc.—these are all things most people will not sacrifice for excellence. It just comes down to your priorities.

I am not saying you cannot ever have these things (except the drinking and drugs), but they should never come at the expense of your goals. At times, it is healthy to allow yourself distractions from school, athletics, work, and other things that demand your focus. Every now and then, you should reward yourself by taking a break and enjoying life beyond sports. You just need to learn how to find *balance* with everything.

Balancing school, your family/social life, and sports can be difficult. It is a lot to handle and they overlap in many ways. If you do poorly in school, you will be ineligible for sports. If you do poorly in sports, your schoolwork and social life might struggle.

On the other hand, if you have success in athletics, it will usually bring you more attention and additional social demands. Suddenly, you might feel obligated to give attention to those who want it. There is an understandable fear of backlash if you do not keep up with social and social media demands.

Please remember, though…there is only so much of you to go around. The faster you learn that you cannot keep everyone happy, the better your life will be. It does not mean you need to be rude to others just because they want to get close to you. Just make sure you are not spreading yourself too thin.

There are hundreds of *things* that will distract you from your goals—each and every day. Things that are fun in the *moment*, but end up being a waste of time—leaving you with regrets. Do you want to know what the biggest waste of time is? *Regret*.

I have never heard of anyone looking back and wishing they played more video games or spent more time on social media. People always have regrets about missed opportunities. Do not sacrifice a lifetime of satisfaction for a moment of gratification.

Another form of distraction that can be difficult to avoid is the media. Let's be real…it is awesome having your name mentioned on TV and the radio, or to read your name in print and online. You work hard, so when you receive accolades, it feels good—you earned it, right?

However, I have to mention that it can become a distraction if you let too much praise go to your head. An overinflated ego is almost always a bad thing. You begin to think you are better than others and you might get lazy in your work ethic. Do not let recognition give you a false sense of security. Keep busting your butt to be great.

On the opposite side of the spectrum, when you receive criticism, it really becomes a difficult distraction. Maybe you made a mistake in a game that cost the team. Maybe people do not think you deserve to be a starter. Maybe you got in trouble off the field. In athletics, there is a very small margin of error that is allowed before people start criticizing you.

Social media is just that—a platform for everyone with Internet or a cell phone to voice their opinions. Everyone now has the ability to try and knock you down. Even if most would disagree with what they say, they can easily take shots at you and inflict damage.

If you let the opinion of every critic, hater, and disgruntled fan get to you, it will wreak havoc on your mentality. And I can guarantee you that you will not last long as a competitor. The best thing you can do when you receive praise or criticism, is to have a short memory and thick skin.

If you want to avoid a lot of frustration/stress and also prevent yourself from getting an inflated ego, do not listen to what other people have to say about you. It sounds corny, but if you can look yourself in the mirror and be proud, that is all that matters.

When it comes to making sure you are not giving in to distractions too much, you should be implementing the techniques we talked about in previous chapters. If the things that severely distract you are part of your routine, nothing will change. Remember, you become the habits you keep.

Giving in to distractions too often means you have a lack of self-discipline. If this is the case, you will never reach the elite level that eludes so many who want to reach it. The payoff for achieving your goals feels so good because you have been denying yourself other pleasures. If it were easy, there would be a lot more successful people in the world.

WHAT OTHERS SAY ABOUT
DISTRACTIONS

"You cannot let praise or criticism get to you. It is a weakness to get caught up in either one." —John Wooden

"It is not the mountains ahead that wear you out; it is the pebble in your shoe." —Muhammad Ali

"Those who work the hardest, who subject themselves to the strictest discipline, who give up certain pleasurable things in order to achieve a goal, are the happiest." —Brutus Hamilton

"A champion pays an extra price to be better than everyone else." —Bear Bryant

"Excellence is the gradual result of sacrifice." —Pat Riley

"Success will not lower its standards to us. We must raise our standards to success." —Randall R. McBride Jr.

"For of all the sad words of tongue or pen, the saddest are these: 'It might have been.'" —John Greenleaf Whittier

"To be a champion, I think you have to see the big picture. It is not about winning and losing; it is about working hard every day and about thriving on a challenge. It is about embracing the pain that you will experience at the end of a race and not being afraid. I think people think too hard and get afraid of a certain challenge." —Summer Sanders

"Do not dream about success. Get out there and work for it."
—Unknown

"It is not about having enough time; it is about making enough time." —Rachel Birmingham

"Take criticism seriously, but not personally. If there is truth or merit in the criticism, try to learn from it. Otherwise, let it roll right off of you." —Hillary Clinton

"20 years from now, you will be more disappointed by the things you did not do, than the ones you did." —Mark Twain

"I attribute my success to this: I never gave or took an excuse."
—Florence Nightingale

"Study while others are sleeping; work while others are loafing; prepare while others are playing; and dream while others are wishing." —William Arthur Ward

"Forget your excuses. You either want it bad or you do not want it at all." —Unknown

"Time is what we want the most, but what we use the worst."
—William Penn

"Better three hours too soon than a minute too late."
—William Shakespeare

"You can always find a distraction if you are looking for one."
—Tom Kite

"Your results are the product of either personal focus or personal distractions. The choice is yours." —John Di Lemme

"Work is hard. Distractions are plentiful. And time is short."
—Adam Hochschild

"By prevailing overall obstacles and distractions, one may unfailingly arrive at his chosen goal or destination."
—Christopher Columbus

"You cannot do big things if you are distracted by small things." —Unknown

"Do not be on your deathbed someday, having squandered your one chance at life, full of regret because you pursued little distractions instead of big dreams." —Derek Sivers

"We rarely find the answers in the distractions. But oh, what possibilities live within the quiet of focus." —Scott Stabile

"Disconnect from everything long enough to see if it feeds your soul or if it is a distraction. What is deeply connected will always remain." —Maryam Hansaa

"One way to boost our willpower and focus is to manage our distractions, instead of letting them manage us."
—Daniel Goleman

"Thinking is good for your mind, but too much thinking leads to distraction." —E. Habib

9: DISTRACTIONS

MY TOP DISTRACTIONS ARE:

1. _____

2. _____

3. _____

4. _____

5. _____

I BALANCE MY GOALS AND DISTRACTIONS BY:

1. _____

2. _____

3. _____

4. _____

5. _____

Notes

Chapter 10
TRASH TALKING

No matter what you do throughout your athletic career, you are going to experience people who say things to try to get you angry and off your game. Opponents, crowds, writers, random people on social media, and the list goes on. You have to be prepared for it—especially if you want to be the best.

What if you have an opponent who will not stop talking in your ear or you have a really rowdy crowd that is taunting you? Are you able to tune them out? Do they get under your skin? Once they figure out that they can get to you, you are done.

For one thing, they are not going to stop—why would they? Secondly, it is going to be that much more difficult for you to get back in the game because they will be that much more confident. They have got you concentrating on the wrong things.

The same thing goes for dealing with crowds. I know how annoying rowdy crowds can be—especially the student sections. If they get the slightest hint that they are rattling you, it is going to get *much* worse. It is going to be much harder to get your head back in the game and quiet them. Do not ever give them the satisfaction of knowing you are frustrated.

If you pose a threat to someone else, do not be surprised when the verbal assaults begin. As irritating as it can be to have someone running their mouth throughout a competition, you need to think of it as a compliment. The main reason they are doing it is because they cannot beat you on talent alone.

They are threatened and realize they have to compensate for their lack of skill. They are not able to go head-to-head with you, so they make up for it with trash talking. Do not let them get in your head. They have too many deficits and cannot keep up with your strengths! Are you going to let them intimidate you?

I mentioned in the Distractions chapter that you are going to have people saying things online at different times, too. People feel untouchable when they are hiding behind a keyboard, and there is not a thing you can do about it. Anyone can say anything, but only *you* can control your reaction. These people are nothing to you and they do not deserve your attention, so do not even give them the time of day.

There is nothing wrong with standing up for yourself, but do not get into a back-and-forth argument with a bunch of nobodies. The best thing you can do is ignore it and move on. Rise above it and shut them up with your talent on the playing field.

This is especially true for anyone who crosses the line from competitive trash talking to cruel, bigoted, or racist comments. Whether it is an opponent, a spectator, or someone online, they are not worth your time. By saying such derogatory things, those people tell us everything we need to know about them. Do not stoop to their level. You ARE better than them, so BE better than them!

What about trash talking as a competitor? Some of the all-time greats were trash talkers. Muhammad Ali, Mike Tyson, Michael Jordan, Larry Bird, Diana Taurasi, and plenty others. All of these competitors were the greatest for most of their careers, and they all liked to taunt their opponents. It worked for them and they were unapologetic about it.

If you like to do some trash talking to intimidate your opponents, that is fine, too. Plain and simple, it is mental warfare. If you can get into your opponent's head and throw them off their game, this gives you an advantage. Anything that will get them to lose focus of their game plan will be to your benefit.

Your personality type is going to be one of the biggest determining factors for whether or not you like to say things to get under your opponents' skin and irritate them. Trash talking comes in many different forms, and people like Muhammad Ali (and the others) are extreme examples.

You do not have to insult your opponents and compromise your integrity as a person and competitor, just to get an edge. Trash talking can also be subtle. Sometimes all you need to do is poke the bear a little and you will get the desired reaction.

This can mean making a well-timed sarcastic comment, doing a little taunting, or even just smiling. When you are doing well and things are going your way, it does not take much to push your opponent over the edge with their frustration. Just be sure to remember this if you do not have the upper hand and the taunting is directed at you.

At times, you will find that your opponent is the one who initiates the trash talk. I never liked to start it, but if my opponent wanted to get mouthy, I was happy to oblige. Some good repartee makes victory that much more satisfying. Being a fierce competitor and speaking your mind can sometimes go hand-in-hand.

If you can get your opponents to mentally throw in the towel, it will be smooth sailing for you and your team. It is true: most people do not do well under pressure—especially when they have someone in their ear. So, when the opportunity presents itself for you to open your mouth and say something, a wide range of things can be said. You just have to be aware of where you want to land on the scale—humble versus cocky.

If it happens to be the case that you do not mind being the "bad guy," you have to own it. It should come as no surprise that people will dislike you and often retaliate, but you cannot have it both ways. You have to sleep in the bed you make. Just make sure you understand that you will not always get the last word.

Whether you are dishing it or receiving it, trash talking is a part of sports. Some of the greatest rivalries in sports are rooted in competitors bad mouthing each other. Sometimes it makes things more competitive and other times it tarnishes good competition. Regardless, it is never going away, so you need to learn to block it out and/or harness it.

WHAT OTHERS SAY ABOUT *TRASH TALKING*

"There is a stubbornness about me that never can bear to be frightened at the will of others. My courage always rises at every attempt to intimidate me." —Jane Austen

"After a while, you realize that putting your actions where your mouth is, makes you less likely to have to put your money where your mouth is." —Criss Jami

"Often those who criticize others reveal what he himself lacks." —Shannon L. Alder

"Do not be distracted by trash talking. Remember, the only taste of success some people have, is when they take a bite out of you. —Zig Ziglar

"The final proof of greatness lies in being able to endure criticism —Elbert Hubbard

"He who throws dirt, always loses ground. —Unknown

"Any fool can criticize, complain, and condemn—and most fools do. But it takes character and self-control to be understanding and forgiving." —Dale Carnegie

"It is not the critic that counts. Not the man who points out how the strong man stumbles or where the doer of deeds could have done them better. The credit belongs to the man who is actually in the arena." —Theodore Roosevelt

10: TRASH TALKING

"The weaker you are, the louder you bark." —Masashi Kishimoto

"Pessimists calculate the odds. Optimists believe they can overcome them." —Ted Koppel

"For myself, I am an optimist—it does not seem to be much use being anything else." —Winston Churchill

"We each have a choice: To approach life as a creator or a critic, a lover or a hater, a giver or a taker." —Unknown

"Champions believe in themselves, even if no one else does."
—Sugar Ray Robinson

"For every one person who says that you can do it, there will be 99 people who say you cannot. Do not be discouraged by the others—be inspired by the one." —Unknown

"Pay no attention to what the critics say. A statue has never been erected in honor of a critic. —Jean Sibelius

"Do not waste your energy trying to change opinions…Do your thing and do not worry if they do not like it. —Tina Fey

"Work hard for what you want because it will not come to you without a fight. You have to be strong and courageous and know that you can do anything you put your mind to. If someone puts you down or criticizes you, just keep on believing in yourself and turn it into something positive."
—Leah Labelle

"I am thankful for all of those who said 'no' to me. It is because of them I am doing it myself." —Wayne W. Dyer

"When you feel like giving up, just remember that there are a lot of people you still have to prove wrong." —Unknown

"I did not learn to be quiet when I had an opinion. The reason they knew who I was is because I told them." —Ursula Burns

"No matter how good you are, someone is always going to be against you. Never let them be the limit of your success."
—Terry Mark

"The only thing more frustrating than slanderers, is those foolish enough to listen to them." —Criss Jami

"Learn to use criticism as fuel and you will never run out of energy." —Orrin Woodward

"I do not worry about the haters… They are just angry because the truth I speak contradicts the lie they live."
—Steve Maraboli

"Remember, people only rain on your parade because they are jealous of your sun and tired of their shade." —Unknown

"Behind every successful person lies a pack of haters."
—Gloria Tesch

"Insecure people put others down to raise themselves up."
—Habeeb Akande

BENEFITS OF TRASH TALKING:

1. _____

2. _____

3. _____

4. _____

5. _____

CONSEQUENCES OF TRASH TALKING:

1. _____

2. _____

3. _____

4. _____

5. _____

Notes

Chapter 11
COMPOSURE

Maintaining your focus in the heat of battle is easily one of the most important components to success. When the pressure is on and all the chips are on the table, how do you handle it? Well, if you want to be the best, there is only one answer: You have to be calm, cool, and collected. This is *composure*.

Have you ever seen someone achieve victory when they were panicking or getting really angry? It does not happen often. It is easy to make a free-throw in an empty gym, sink a putt when no one is watching, or complete a pass when you are not being rushed. But can you do those things when you are down, all eyes are on you, the crowd is loud, your opponent is jawing in your ear, your adrenaline is pumping, and there is not much time left on the clock?

If you really want to separate yourself from average athletes, you have to be composed under pressure. When Navy SEALs and Army Rangers are going through training, they do it under extreme circumstances so they can learn how to stay calm and focused when lives are on the line. This is why SEALs and Rangers are the ones sent in to do the really difficult missions—they are taught to have ice in their veins.

Sports are not life or death situations; however, just like war, coaches use strategies to achieve victory. If players lose their composure, strategies fall apart and victory is lost. When the pressure is on, can your teammates and coaches count on you?

You can always tell if someone is afraid or confident just by looking in their eyes. Confidence and composure are not things you can just fake and expect everything to work out well. If a player really has composure, you should be able to look him or her in the face and not be able to tell if they are leading their team on a last possession comeback or waiting in line for their food at Chick-fil-A. They are stoic, unflappable, and focused.

If you are trailing late in the game and your teammates look over at you and see that you are composed and ready to bring it, they are going to feed off of that confidence. Alternatively, if they see fear or apprehension, they will start to doubt themselves, too. Composure and concern are both contagious.

Sometimes it is possible to get in your own head and self-destruct. The game plan is not working as well as you expected, you are not performing as well as you usually do, your shots are just not hitting their mark, and many other scenarios can make you hit the panic button. Slow starts and brief funks can and will happen.

If you find yourself in this situation, you have to remind yourself that YOU CAN pull it together and regain your composure. If you have teammates, lean on each other to get the momentum going again and get back on track. Look your coach or your teammates in the eye, pull it together and fight until there is not any time left on the clock.

The best competitors learn how to put these things out of their mind and regroup quickly. Any bad plays that already happened are in the past, so move on and get back in your groove. The old cliché is true: *"It is not how you start; it is how you finish."* Even if you lose, you can hold your head high knowing that you never gave up.

I mentioned it in the last chapter, but when your opponent resorts to trash talking, you have to be able to tune them out. Actions speak louder than words. Keeping your composure will shut your opponent up and quiet a crowd extremely fast.

Do you know how stupid you make others feel when they try to intimidate you, yet you proceed to perform flawlessly? It is a great feeling to watch their confidence and composure crack when they realize they are not going to get to you. If you like to trash talk, make sure you remember this.

Playing with composure also means playing with class. If you get an opponent who plays dirty or says ridiculous things just to get under your skin, it does not mean that you need to give them the reaction they are looking for. Even if they keep it up the entire game, beat them on the playing field and then walk away.

I promise you—they will never forget how insignificant you made them feel when you whooped them and then walked off like a boss. It is the ultimate mic drop and they will feel humiliated because all their efforts failed.

In the event you suffer defeat, make sure you are composed afterwards as well. It is never fun to lose, but do not ever let your emotions boil over and cause insult to injury. Shake hands with your opponents and wait until you get into the locker room. Especially nowadays where everyone has a camera, you do not want to go down in history for the way you behave after a loss.

Building upon the other components we discussed in previous chapters, composure is something that comes with experience and only happens when you combine a lot of other mentality traits. You have to practice, train, study, and prepare to the point that you are ready for whatever gets thrown at you.

Mouthy opponent? No problem. Rowdy crowd? Cannot even hear them. Terrible referees? Does not matter. Your opponent hits a hot streak and pulls way ahead? Watch this comeback. None of these things can touch you if you are mentally *in the zone*. Never forget the 6 Cs: Calm, cool, and composed competitors collect championships.

WHAT OTHERS SAY ABOUT *COMPOSURE*

"When we long for life without difficulties, remind us that oaks grow strong in contrary winds, and diamonds are made under pressure." —Peter Marshall

"You are never really playing an opponent. You are playing yourself, your own highest standards, and when you surpass your perceived limits, that is real joy." —Arthur Ashe

"In the long run, the pessimist may be proved right, but the optimist has a better time on the trip." —Daniel L. Reardon

"You were born to be a player. You were meant to be here. This moment is yours." —Herb Brooks

"Trust yourself that you can do it and get it." —Baz Luhrmann

"My father taught me in boxing, that when you get hit in the face for the first time, you are going to panic. That, instead of panicking, just accept it. Stay calm. And any time anybody hits you, they always leave themselves open to be hit."
—Rudy Giuliani

"A diamond is merely a lump of coal that did well under pressure." —Unknown

"At the end of the day, we can endure much more than we think we can." —Frida Kahlo

11: COMPOSURE

"Life is 10% what happens to you and 90% how you react to it." —Charles Swindoll

"When the pain of an obstacle is too great, challenge yourself to be stronger." —Unknown

"Always keep your composure. You cannot score from the penalty box." —Bobby Hull

"The beauty of the soul shines out when a person bears with composure, one heavy misfortune after another. Not because he does not feel them, but because he is a person of high and heroic temperament." —Aristotle

"Every great player has learned the two C's: how to concentrate and how to maintain composure." —Byron Nelson

"It is about being smart, taking your time, keeping your composure, just going out there and being the best you can be."
—Floyd Mayweather, Jr.

"You must keep your composure. Take charge of the huddle. Be a leader. And silence the crowd." —Eric Thomas

"Losing composure is pointless." —Michael Schumacher

"Controlled aggression, to me, is one of the most important traits to have. To have that social intelligence to know when to exert aggression in the military environment, and when to stay calm, cool, and collected." —Johnny Kim

"I know I perform my best when I stay calm."
—Shikhar Dhawan

"When I play, I am boiling inside. I just try not to show it because it is a lack of composure, and if you give in to your emotions after one loss, you are liable to have three or four in a row." —Chris Evert

"When I joined the Tour, I studied the best players to see what they did that I did not do. I came to the conclusion that the successful players had the three C's: confidence, composure, concentration." —Bob Toski

"Breaking composure, confidence, and speed in the water makes you lose the race—not the goggles that fell off your head when you dove in." —Amanda Beard

"People ask me what makes a great skier. It takes the gift; but besides the gift it takes all the availability of mind which permit total control of all the elements that lead to victory—total composure." —Jean-Claude Killy

"Mistakes and pressure are inevitable; the secret to getting past them is to stay calm." —Travis Bradbery

"Win or lose, just stay calm." —Mirko Cro Cop

"Losing your composure is like a rocking chair. It gives you something to do, but it does not get you very far."
—Jodi Picoult

SITUATIONS I REMEMBER LOSING MY COMPOSURE:

1.

2.

3.

4.

5.

I CAN REGAIN/MAINTAIN MY COMPOSURE BY:

1.

2.

3.

4.

5.

Notes

Chapter 12
ATTITUDE

Composure is what you need when you are in the midst of adversity. A good *attitude* is what you need once the dust settles. The importance of attitude cannot be understated. In athletics and everything else in life, attitude is everything. You cannot always control what happens to you or around you, but you can always control how you respond.

Did not win? Should you put it behind you and focus on your next opponent—or stay mad and consider the season over? Got injured? Take rehab head-on—or be negative and put your athletic career in your rearview? Did not get the starting job? Keep working hard and wait for another opportunity to prove yourself—or sulk on the sidelines and be a distraction for everyone else? These are ALL choices of attitude.

Just like creating routines has to be a habit, having a good attitude has to become a habit as well. It is not always easy to do, but anyone can do it. It just takes practice and consistency. If you can practice your form, technique, or mechanics, you can practice your attitude.

When adversity happens, you have to train yourself to respond positively. Not only will it help you get through things faster, but other people will feed off of your positivity and have a better attitude as well. Everything is easier when you have a good attitude.

Please understand that I am not trying to say you are a bad person if you get upset, angry, frustrated, etc. To play sports, you have to be emotionally invested. The greatest competitors are always passionate.

But do not confuse being passionate with having a bad attitude simply because things did not work out the way you had hoped. Vent and get your emotions out, but then move *forward*.

This is especially true in team sports. It is one thing if you are a golfer and have a bad attitude. It is a whole different issue if your attitude brings your teammates down with you. If you make a bad play and give up some points to the other team, you can either choose to acknowledge it and make up for it, or make a scene and distract your team.

When your teammates have to pull their focus from the game in order to calm you down and convince you that it is "OK," all you are doing is making a bad situation worse. I get really annoyed whenever I see a player make a mistake in a game and then proceed to hang their head or be really dramatic on the sideline. It is like they believe it makes things better, but they actually end up hurting the team more.

Mistakes are going to happen! The first thing you have to do is start thinking positively and override any negative thoughts. If things are not going well for you, shutting down or losing your focus is not going to help your situation.

These points also apply to athletes playing individual sports. You already know that it is just you out there and if things start to go off the rails, only you can pull yourself out of the funk. Yes, you can still look over to your coach for some reassurance and guidance, but ultimately, the choice of attitude has to come from within you.

Your coach may yell at you for making a bad play or screwing up, but he or she will not appreciate any kind of bad attitude in response. Getting yelled at is never fun, but you cannot take it personally. This needs repeated...YOU CANNOT TAKE IT PERSONALLY! Players who can get over it quickly are always the ones who end up being great.

The best way to handle the situation is to own it and tell your coach or teammates you will make up for it—never self-destruct. If you do get yelled at, listen to what your coach tells you, acknowledge your mistake and move on. Carry your own weight and do not make your team do it for you. If your attitude brings your team down, you are only helping your opponent.

Any athlete with a good attitude is coachable. When you are coachable, it means your coach is going to be excited to pour their knowledge into you. Soak all that in because it is only going to make you better all around. Coaches will avoid helping you if they know it is just going to lead to dealing with your poor attitude.

Do not develop a reputation for being a hothead, either. People are always watching. Coaches, teammates, opponents, the crowd, etc. It is a pretty safe bet to assume that anyone who is quick to have a bad attitude, is not very good at keeping his or her composure. Once people find out you are easily rattled, your coaches/teammates will lose their trust in you and your opponents will use it to their advantage.

Not only is it important to have the right attitude when things are not going well, it is important to win gracefully, too. Defeating an opponent will give you an opportunity to either insult them and throw it in their face, or to shake their hand and acknowledge the effort they put in. Be the latter.

If they choose to be a sore loser, it should not affect your ability to be respectful towards them. Let them have the bad attitude. Others will notice that you handle things with class, which will earn you their respect.

Having the right attitude can be a difficult thing to master. It is a process and it takes time and effort to figure out. The most important thing is to always be learning from your mistakes. As you learn, you will understand that attitude is a choice.

Deciding to have a good or a bad attitude is one of the most important decisions you will have to make on a regular basis as an athlete and as a person. I can guarantee you with 100% certainty that if you choose to have a bad attitude, it will be impossible for you to perform to the best of your ability. The choice is yours.

WHAT OTHERS SAY ABOUT
ATTITUDE

"A loser says, 'It may be possible, but it will be difficult.' A winner says, 'It may be difficult, but it is possible.'" —Unknown

"Be dissatisfied enough to improve, but satisfied enough to be happy." —J. Harold Smith

"Attitude is the mind's paintbrush… Create a masterpiece!" —John Maxwell

"Most people are about as happy as they make their minds to be." —Abraham Lincoln

"The greatest discovery is that a human being can alter his life by altering his attitude of mind." —William James

"Always bear in mind that your own resolution to succeed is more important than any one thing." —Abraham Lincoln

"A strong positive attitude will create more miracles than any drug." —Patricia Neal

"Our minds can shape the way a thing will be, because we act according to our expectations." —Federico Fellini

"Weakness of attitude becomes weakness of character." —Albert Einstein

12: ATTITUDE

"We are what we think. All that we are arises with our thoughts. With our thoughts, we make our world." —Buddha

"You cannot have a long, successful career without a positive attitude. I believe that an I-can-do-anything mentality is the competitor's best friend." —Nolan Ryan

"If we have the attitude that it is going to be a great day, it usually is." —Catherine Pulsifier

"Doubt kills more dreams than failure every well."
—Suzy Kassem

"You are so much stronger than your excuses." —Unknown

"I can be changed by what happens to me. But I refuse to be reduced by it." —Maya Angelou

"The problem is not the problem. The problem is your attitude about the problem." —Unknown

"You can control two things: your work ethic and your attitude about anything." —Ali Krieger

"Your positive action combined with positive thinking results in success." —Shiv Khera

"Why do we grieve failures longer than we celebrate wins?"
—Komal Kapor

"A negative mind will never give you a positive life."
—Lewis Hamilton

"Attitude is everything, so pick a good one." —Wayne Dyer

"Attitude is a little thing that makes a big difference."
—Winston Churchill

Your attitude, not your aptitude, determines your altitude."
—Zig Ziglar

"Excellence is not a skill; it is an attitude." —Ralph Marston

"Two things define you: your patience when you have nothing and your attitude when you have everything."
—George Bernard Shaw

"It is our attitude at the beginning of a difficult task which, more than anything else, will affect its successful outcome."
—William James

"I believe the single most significant decision I can make on a day-to-day basis, is my choice of attitude." —Charles Swindoll

"The attitude is very important because your behavior radiates how you feel." —Lou Ferrigno

"The greatest day in your life and mine is when we take total responsibility for our attitudes. That is the day we truly grow up." —John C. Maxwell

LESSONS I HAVE LEARNED WHEN I HAD A POOR ATTITUDE:

1.
2.
3.
4.
5.

TIMES MY/MY TEAMMATE'S BAD ATTITUDE MADE THINGS WORSE:

1.
2.
3.
4.
5.

Notes

Chapter 13

WHAT IF?

Taking what we discussed about composure and attitude, now it is time to talk about how you will maintain them when things are not going well. Sure, it is important to understand your opponent if you want to win, but it is just as important to understand *yourself*. In this chapter, we are going to preemptively address how you should respond in difficult situations.

If you can learn to handle adversity with composure and a good attitude, the likelihood of success will skyrocket. A chain is only as strong as its weakest link. Well, do not let your mentality be your weak link. Being mentally prepared for any and all situations means running through different scenarios and determining how you would react.

Businesses have contingency plans so they can be prepared for hard times—if there is a downturn in the market, if employees strike, if there are production issues, and an endless number of other "what if" scenarios. The more you can mentally prepare for adverse situations, the better you will handle them in the heat of the moment.

Here are some "what if" scenarios you should consider and also talk through with your teammates and/or your coach:

- What if teammates start arguing during a game?
- What if a referee makes a bad call and it causes a big setback?
- What if your opponent is doing a lot of trash talking?
- What if you make a big mistake during a critical part of the game?
- What if the other team rallies and now you are behind late in the game?

- What if the other team is playing dirty?
- What if you lose a key player in the middle of a competition?
- What if you lose to an opponent you should have easily beaten?

On one hand, the answers to all of the scenarios I listed are obvious: *do not self-destruct.* However, just because you know the answer to the question, does not mean everyone involved will suddenly be able to execute it if you find yourself in one of these situations. This is especially true when the stakes are high and everything is on the line.

What other "what if" situations can you come up with that would be beneficial to address ahead of time? Your coach should be taking the time to rehearse scenarios like the ones listed above. The only way for you to begin to know how to respond in certain circumstances, is to practice them.

At Ohio State, we had time set aside for *situational preparation* multiple days a week. For example: *37 seconds left, one timeout, 2nd and 11 from the 40-yard line, we are down by a field goal and our starting QB just went down with an injury—Now, handle it.*

By the way, we had huge speakers around the practice field and they would blast loud crowd noise to make it harder to communicate. Sometimes, coaches would sneak up with water bottles and spray players right before the ball was snapped, just to try to throw them off. You have to be able to think clearly under pressure.

There is only so much time to process information, focus, and execute during a competition when things get stressful. Depending on the sport you play or situation you are in, you may not even get to take a timeout in order to talk things over. Whatever the case, establishing a protocol ahead of time will help de-escalate a situation where you need to pull things together and avoid imploding.

So, what do I mean by this? For starters, as a team, you all need to understand who is calling the shots on the playing field and who needs to listen. There is never time to argue. Everyone should know ahead of time what has to be done in any given scenario, so everyone can execute and win.

Secondly, you should have a *focus phrase* (some call it a mantra), that you and/or your teammates adopt as a way of mentally resetting when things are not going your way. It can be a word, a signal, or anything that lets you know you need to take a deep breath and move past whatever is holding you back in that situation. Things will not automatically start improving, but the best way to get out of a funk is to mentally refocus and move forward.

Having an understanding of all the outcomes means being realistic that bad things happen sometimes. This does not mean you should plan on things going wrong, but it does mean you should be prepared when they do. How are you going to *choose* to respond when doubts start to creep in and everything you have worked for is on the line?

As a quick side note, I want to make sure you understand that there is a difference between *worrying* about these details and *preparing* for them. There should be no sense of worry or stress when it comes to handling challenging scenarios. This is all meant to make you a better competitor, because you will be ready to handle whatever is thrown at you. I want you to learn to react with composure instead of panic.

It may not be easy to think about the negative side of things, but it is necessary. Sure, there is no way to rehearse or prepare for every bad thing that might happen. However, if you can process through these scenarios and more, you are going to be much better equipped to come out on top—no matter what.

WHAT OTHERS SAY ABOUT "WHAT IF"

"I have learned that something constructive comes from every defeat." —Tom Landry

"Adversity causes some men to break; others to break records." —William Arthur Ward

"If you never stick your neck out, you will never get your head above the crowd." —Unknown

"Learn from the mistakes of others, you cannot live long enough to make them all yourself." —Martin Vanbee

"Why not go out on a limb? Is not that where all the fruit is?" —Frank Scully

"If you keep on saying things are going to be bad, you have a good chance of being a prophet." —Isaac Bashevis Singer

"The same boiling water that softens the potato, hardens the egg. It is what you are made of, not the circumstances." —Unknown

"I always did something I was a little not ready to do. I think that is how you grow. When there is that moment of 'Wow, I am not really sure I can do this,' and you push through those moments, that is when you have a breakthrough." —Marissa Mayer

"I can and I will. Watch me." —Carrie Green

"What is life without a little risk?" —J.K. Rowling

"Falling down is how we grow. Staying down is how we die."
—Brian Vaszily

"You may be disappointed if you fail, but you will be doomed if you do not try." —Beverly Sills

"Failure is the tuition you pay for success." —Walter Brunel

"You cannot let your failures define you. You have to let your failures teach you." —Barack Obama

"Never regret a day in your life. Good days bring you happiness and bad days give you experience." —Unknown

"I cannot change the direction of the wind, but I can adjust my sails to always reach my destination." —Jimmy Dean

"Ever notice the word 'rough' in through? There is truth to that. Though the way may be rough, we are still able to get through it." —Anthony Liccione

"Courage is the most important of all the virtues because without courage, you cannot practice any other virtue consistently." —Maya Angelou

"Keep going. Your hardest times often lead to the greatest moments of your life. Keep going. Tough situations build strong people in the end." —Roy T. Bennett

"One setback does not have to rule any person's entire life."
—Joyce Meyer

"Character consists of what you do on the third and fourth tries." —James Michener

"It is better to take many small steps in the right direction, than to make a great leap in the wrong direction."
—Louis Sachar

"We are made to persist—that is how we find out who we are." —Tobias Wolff

"We love being mentally strong, but we hate situations that allow us to put our mental strength to good use."
—Mokokoma Mokhonoana

"Success does not come to you; you go to it." —T. Scott McLeod

"If the fire in your heart is strong enough, it will burn away any obstacles that come your way." —Suzy Kassem

"To persist with a goal, you must treasure the dream more than the costs of sacrifice to attain it." —Richelle Goodrich

SCENARIOS IN WHICH I OR SOMEONE ELSE RESPONDED POORLY:

1. _____

2. _____

3. _____

4. _____

5. _____

SCENARIOS IN WHICH I OR SOMEONE ELSE RESPONDED CORRECTLY:

1. _____

2. _____

3. _____

4. _____

5. _____

Notes

Chapter 14
LEADERSHIP & RESPONSIBILITY

All the chapters up to this point have focused on making you a better competitor. Once you put everything together, your skillset should be above and beyond your competition. When that happens, your coach will most likely put you in a *leadership* position.

Teammates will look up to you and your coach will want them to follow your example. Regardless of whether you want to be the one who throws the team on your back and carry everyone to the finish line, or if you would rather be in a supportive role, leadership is needed on every level. EVERY role is important.

The military is the ultimate example of how leadership works. Commands come from the top general (coach), to be carried out by the colonels (captains), who rely on the majors (seniors/juniors) to lead the troops (underclassmen) on the battlefield. Everyone needs to understand their role and how to work together. This is how game plans end up being successful.

No matter where you fall in the chain of command, you should always be trying to elevate your teammates' level of play. A rising tide lifts all boats. Even if you are not a captain, you can still set an example and do exactly what is needed. Team captains need to depend upon their teammates, so do not slack on your duties.

Any good leader needs to have good character. Your true character is who you are when no one is watching. If you are in a leadership position, can your coaches and teammates depend on you to represent the program with class and integrity? With great power, comes great responsibility! Do not let everyone down by doing something that will hurt the team.

One of the most important things you can do if you want to be a great leader, is encourage your teammates so they grow in confidence. The best leaders can inspire others to achieve more than they think they are capable of. Build others up and watch how much the team thrives!

I came across a great quote that uniquely states how profound a leadership role is: "*They say adversity shows your true character. Well, I believe people are actually pretty well-suited to handle adversity. If you really want to test someone's character, put them in a leadership role and see how he or she handles it*" —Unknown.

Have you ever had teammates who were in a leadership position and you resented them because they expected everyone else to bow down to them? Have you ever been this kind of teammate? Anyone who wants to be a good leader needs to carefully consider this. You should never be foolish enough to believe you do not have room to improve as a leader.

Just like respect, leadership is earned. If you are a senior or a captain, you have *authority*. But, if you have to declare your authority, you are failing as a leader. A good leader never has to demand the respect of his or her team. They always lead by example. If you demonstrate your authority and leadership with respect and character, the rest will fall into place.

Your team will look to you to gauge how they should respond in different situations. If you lose your cool, team composure crumbles, too. You will be amazed at how much better people do when you encourage them instead of yell at them. A good leader always knows how to communicate constructively—which is covered in the next chapter.

If you are an underclassman, most of your time should be spent listening and learning. However, you can still contribute by working hard and helping other underclassmen. If your coach feels you are mature enough and talented enough, he or she may give you more responsibilities and more playing time. This may seem a little daunting at first, but step up to the challenge and raise your level of play. Leaders come in all shapes and sizes!

It is extremely important to be a leader off the field, too. Lead by example and speak up if you see teammates doing things in class or out on the weekend that could jeopardize the team. This can be a difficult thing to do, but you do not want to live with regret because you or a teammate chose to do something stupid.

Someone is always watching—especially with cameras being everywhere nowadays. Do you really want to jeopardize the team or your future for one lapse in judgment? One bad decision is all it takes. Sometimes it is someone who is just waiting for you to slip up so they can watch you suffer the consequences. As a leader, it is your responsibility to do the right thing and make sure your teammates do, too.

Being responsible is not always fun, but it is always necessary. Not only are people watching and waiting for you to slip up, there are also people watching you to learn how to do things *the right way*. You do not even have to be an upperclassman…There are a lot of younger, impressionable people looking up to you. Show them what a real leader looks like!

You probably do not even realize it most of the time, but they are there—observing what you say and do. Set an example that they will carry on even after you are gone. One of the best compliments you will ever receive is when someone comes up to you years down the line and tells you that you made a positive impact on him or her, yet you never even realized it at the time.

When a team has leaders from top to bottom, success always follows. If you want to be the best, you have to have leadership and responsibility; there is no getting around this. Embrace it and be a role model for others to do the same!

WHAT OTHERS SAY ABOUT *LEADERSHIP & RESPONSIBILITY*

"Talent is God-given. Be humble. Fame is man-given. Be grateful. Conceit is self-given. Be careful." —John Wooden

"Progress always involves risk. You cannot steal second base and keep your foot on first base." —Frederick Wilcox

"When nobody around you seems to measure up, it is time to check your yard stick." —Bill Lemley

"It is not fair to ask of others, what you are not willing to do yourself." —Eleanor Roosevelt

"You cannot live a perfect day without doing something for someone who will never be able to repay you." —John Wooden

"You can easily judge the character of a man by how he treats those who can do nothing for him." —Malcolm S. Forbes

"Power is the ability to do good for others." —Brooke Astor

"I have always tried to lead by example—never by talking, because words do not mean as much as action. They always say a picture is worth 1000 words. So, I try to paint a picture of hard work and discipline." —Michael Jordan

"A man must be big enough to admit his mistakes, smart enough to profit from them, and strong enough to correct them." —John C. Maxwell

"Leaders can let you fail and yet not let you be a failure."
—Stanley McChrystal

"Do not think or judge, just listen." —Sarah Dessen

"The world is changed by your example, not by your opinion."
—Paulo Coelho

"The greatest gift you could give someone is your time. Because when you give your time, you are giving a portion of your life you cannot get back." —Unknown

"Everything is hard before it is easy." —Goethe

"Management is doing things right; leadership is doing the right things." —Peter F. Drucker

"Stay calm and be quick on fixing the problem. Stopping a problem head-on is vital to running a team." —Monica Galetti

"You cannot escape the responsibilities of tomorrow by evading it today." —Abraham Lincoln

"Our chief want is someone who will inspire us to be what we know we could be." —Ralph Waldo Emerson

"The price of greatness is responsibility." —Winston Churchill

"The mediocre teacher tells. The good teacher explains. The superior teacher demonstrates. The great teacher inspires."
—William Arthur Ward

"Those who enjoy responsibility usually get it; those who merely like exercising authority usually lose it."
—Malcolm Forbes

"The greatest leader is not necessarily the one who does the greatest things. It is the one that gets the people to do the greatest things." —Ronald Reagan

"There is a single reason why 99 out of 100 average businessmen and women never become leaders. That is their unwillingness to pay the price of responsibility. By the price of responsibility, I mean hard-driving, continual work and doing what is right." —Owen Young

"Leaders must be close enough to relate to others, but far enough ahead to motivate them." —John C. Maxwell

"There is a difference between being a leader and being a boss. Both are based on authority. A boss demands blind obedience; a leader earns their authority through understanding and trust." —Klaus Balkenhol

"Leadership is an action, not a position." —Donald McGannon

"If your actions do not live up to your words, you have nothing to say." —DaShanne Stokes

"If you want to build a ship, do not drum up the men to gather wood, divide the work, and give orders. Instead, inspire them to yearn for the vast and endless sea."
—Antoine de Saint Exupery

A GOOD LEADER SHOULD:

1. _____

2. _____

3. _____

4. _____

5. _____

A BAD LEADER WILL:

1. _____

2. _____

3. _____

4. _____

5. _____

Notes

Chapter 15

COMMUNICATION

As obvious as it seems, people do not realize just how important *communication* is when working together as a team. Your ability to communicate and be on the same page as your coach and/or teammates will increase your ability to win. The moment communication breaks down, people start doing their own thing and the gameplan goes out the window.

You might be wondering, *"What does this have to do with my mentality?"* All of the mentality strategies we have covered so far have been for your *personal* benefit. Your communication skills should raise your teammates' level of play, which obviously benefits *them*. This is another characteristic of what winners do.

I mentioned in the last chapter that you will always end up in a leadership role when you become one of the best players. With that in mind, you are going to need to communicate well with your coaches and teammates. Your coach will expect you to help with making sure things run smoothly in practice and in games.

If you want to be a great communicator, you first need to be a good listener. Barking out orders and not listening to your coach or teammates leads to frustration. This will turn into resentment and things never go well when that happens. If people see you are willing to hear them out and listen, they will feel more respected and more willing to follow you as a leader.

The most beneficial result of good communication is team cohesiveness. Look at every championship team in any sport, at any level and you will see that they all communicate as a unit. There is no division amongst the team—no fighting and no confusion as to what the game plan is. If there is, the leaders step up and figure it out in a calm and assertive way.

A crucial component to efficient communication for a team is *terminology*. The terminology you use is like your own specific language, and language is the foundation of communication. If everyone is speaking the same language, you can openly communicate on the playing field without your opponent knowing what you are saying.

This is why elite level teams will have a "comms book," which lists all the special words (play names, audibles, shifts, alerts, etc.) and defines what they mean. All players and coaches should be fluent when it comes to terminology, so everyone is on the same page.

When everyone on a team is communicating together, anyone watching can see it clear as day. The efficiency, the ease, and the effectiveness all help create an additional advantage that will make a lot of opponents hit the panic button. This is one of the most valuable aspects of communication.

Even if you play an individual sport, you still need to speak the same language as your coach, so you can work through any problems that arise. You should be able to convey what you are seeing and experiencing on the field of play, so your coach can give you the best guidance possible during a competition. That way, you can make adjustments to your game plan and tweak your strategy.

The coach/player relationship is extremely important and communication is vital to its success. A big part of it relies on trust, which only comes with open communication. A good coach should always be receptive to feedback and the same is true for the athlete. If you communicate well with your coach, things will go much more smoothly.

Communication can break down for a number of reasons. One of the main reasons is because too many people decide that they know best, so they refuse to listen to others. This is straight up selfishness. If you are a captain or a team leader and you realize this is happening, you need to put a stop to it right away. Everyone deserves to be heard, but it cannot happen if people refuse to listen.

Another common cause for communication breaking down is because of a lack of respect. I mentioned in the last chapter that good leaders should never have to assert their authority. Respect is earned, not demanded. If you treat others respectfully and listen when they have things to say, communication works a lot better.

The last threat to communication I want to address, is the tone in which you talk. Sometimes we do not realize that we sound condescending or that we can come across a little too aggressively. This can happen easily in sports because competitors are passionate. When you are playing aggressively, whether it is practice or a game, it is difficult to stop and talk in a calm tone if something happens.

As a good communicator, you have to be aware of how you sound. Nobody likes to get yelled at. When constructive criticism is necessary, speak in a way that makes those involved feel like they are on your level. That is how your message is most likely to be heard.

One of the best ways to create better team communication is through trust and respect. Team building exercises are a great tool to use and you have probably done them without even realizing. Off-season workouts, partnering up in the weight room, a fun team competition, a team trip to a local pool or a cookout are all examples.

When teams are filled with players who trust each other and communicate effectively, it is like a well-oiled machine. Things run smoothly because everyone is able to anticipate each other and make adjustments quickly—if needed. This only comes after hours and hours of being around each other (on and off the field of play). When it happens, it is a beautiful thing. Never forget that communication is the answer to the problem, and the problem to the answer.

WHAT OTHERS SAY ABOUT *COMMUNICATION*

"Raise your words, not your voice. It is rain that grows flowers, not thunder." —Rumi

"We have two ears and one mouth so we can listen twice as much as we speak." —Epictetus

"Communication is a skill that you can learn. It is like riding a bicycle or typing. If you are willing to work at it, you can rapidly improve the quality of every part of your life."
—Brian Tracy

"Wise men speak because they have something to say; fools because they have to say something." —Unknown

"Half the world is composed of people who have something to say and cannot, and the other half who have nothing to say and keep on saying it." —Robert Frost

"Communication—the human connection—is the key to personal and career success." —Paul J. Meyer

"Take advantage of every opportunity to practice your communication skills, so that when important occasions arise, you will have the gift, the style, the sharpness, the clarity, and the emotions to affect other people." —Jim Rohn

"There is only one rule for being a good talker: learn to listen."
—Christopher Morley

15: COMMUNICATION

"Communication leads to community; that is, to understanding, intimacy, and mutual valuing." —Rollo May

"Words are singularly the most powerful force available to humanity. We can choose to use this force constructively with words of encouragement, or destructively using words of despair. Words have energy and power with the ability to help, to heal, to hinder, to hurt, to harm, to humiliate, and to humble." —Yehuda Berg

"The most important thing in communication is hearing what is not said." —Peter Drucker

"To communicate effectively, we must realize that we are all different in the way we perceive the world and use this understanding as a guide to our communication with others."
—Tony Robbins

"Whatever words we utter should be chosen with care. For people will hear them and be influenced by them, for good or ill." —Buddha

"The two words 'information' and 'communication' are often used interchangeably, but they signify quite different things. Information is given out; communication is getting through."
—Sydney Harris

"Words—so innocent and powerless as they are, as standing in a dictionary—how potent for good and evil they become in the hands of one who knows how to combine them."
—Nathaniel Hawthorne

"The game of life is a game of boomerangs. Our thoughts, deeds, and words return to us sooner or later with astounding accuracy." —Florence Scovel Shinn

"Genius is the ability to put into effect what is in your mind."
—F. Scott Fitzgerald

"Communication works for those who work at it."
—John Powell

"The single biggest problem in communication is the illusion that it has taken place." —George Bernard Shaw

"Effective communication helps to keep the team working on the right projects with the right attitude." —Alex Langer

"If people had the right skills and intention to communicate well, there would be no conflict. The better we are communicating, the better our lives will be." —Yama Mubtaker

"The art of communication is the language of leadership."
—James Humes

"Good communication is the bridge between confusion and clarity." —Nat Turner

"Bad communication ends a lot of good things. Good communication ends a lot of bad things." —Unknown

GOOD COMMUNICATION ENABLES A TEAM TO:

1.

2.

3.

4.

5.

A BAD COMMUNICATOR WILL:

1.

2.

3.

4.

5.

Notes

Chapter 16

RELOADING

When you are a student-athlete, a major component to starting each new season is filling the spots of those who have moved on. Whether it is seniors who graduated, teammates who have transferred to other schools, or those who have worked hard enough to achieve their dream of playing at the next level, this means only one thing for those who remain: *opportunity*.

Just like everything else, there is a routine for starting every new season. Elite level programs call it *reloading*. If you want a starting job or leadership role, prove that you deserve it. Everyone from top to bottom needs to step up and take on their new roles. Whatever happened last year is done, so take advantage of this opportunity or someone else will. New leaders, new energy, new expectations. Use all of these things as motivation to reinvigorate yourself and your teammates to achieve all of your goals.

If you happened to come up short last year and did not quite meet the expectations you had hoped for, it can be really tough to put it behind you and refocus. If you truly want to come back with a vengeance and take what is rightfully yours, you need to reflect and learn from your successes and failures.

Everyone involved needs to share their thoughts on what they believe worked well, what did not, and how things can be improved. This process is very similar to what we discussed in Strengths and Deficits. Fresh and strategic game plans need to be implemented each year, based on what your team or individual strengths are. Your coach(es) should discuss this with the team and have open communication. Having everyone on the same page about this will help you use it to your advantage.

If you are truly dissatisfied with previous results, you need to let that be your driving force. It needs to be a hunger that cannot be satisfied and a thirst that cannot be quenched until you are holding that trophy above your head. By this point, you should have reminders posted all over your room, bathroom, fridge, phone, car, locker, and everywhere else you can think of. You are on a *mission*.

Shifting gears...If you were fortunate enough to win a championship last year, congratulations! However, you are not given a whole lot of time to enjoy it before you have to look out for people trying to knock you off. If you did not have a bullseye on your back before, there is no hiding anymore. You are now the main target on everyone's radar.

You cannot fully understand it until you get there, but everything looks totally different when you are standing at the top of the mountain, looking down at everyone and everything else. This perspective is a heck of a thing.

After you have taken a little time to celebrate and soak it all in, you also need to reflect on the journey and what it took to attain your dream. What areas can you learn from and improve upon? Are you ready to do it all over again? All the commitment, sacrifice, blood, sweat, and tears?

The answer is obviously, "*YES!*" This is who you are and once you get a taste of success, you will want more of it. Like I mentioned before, victory makes all of the sacrifices worth it. You will find out soon enough if you are up for the challenge.

Thankfully, you do not have to reinvent yourself. You have the recipe for greatness—now how do we make it better? Typically, the best place to start is by figuring out what the deficits are. Learn from your mistakes and eliminate them. You have to do this because everyone else will adapt so they can try to bring you down.

They will study you. They will analyze your game film to find your flaws. They will come up with new schemes to make it harder for you to win—whatever it takes to knock you off the throne. So how are you going to improve in order to stay on top?

Secondly, a great strategy is to find out what you did well and make it even better. Businesses will do this a lot. They will play to their strengths and focus on their bread and butter, so they can keep smashing their competition. You should still try to eliminate any flaws in your game, but my point is, do not neglect what works well for you.

The thing you need to remember about greatness is there is no single recipe. However, the ingredients you need to be great are always consistent: Discipline, class, enthusiasm, focus, humility, persistence, accountability, toughness, etc. You have to be intentional if you want to be great.

None of these things will just suddenly be added to your repertoire unless you make a conscious effort. Do not make the mistake of thinking that you cannot add more ingredients or improve upon the ones you have. Achieving your goals did not just fall into your lap, so why should things be any different even after you attain greatness?

Reloading and maintaining the same level of work ethic and dedication can be difficult after reaching the top. This is why you do not see very many individuals or teams repeat multiple championships. A big reason for this is because they start to convince themselves that they can take the day off or not work as hard, because they "know what they are doing."

We touched on this when we talked about confidence. Do not become overconfident and start thinking you will not have to put in the work in order to continue winning. This would not only be ignorant and arrogant; it would be a HUGE mistake!

Never become complacent. The moment you take your foot off the gas, your competition will catch up to you and you will get passed. You are either reading this as someone who wants to knock off the current reigning champion, or you are the reigning champion and you want to protect your crown. Whatever the scenario is, it just comes down to who is hungrier.

Kenyon College is a division III school in central Ohio that most people have never heard of. Why am I mentioning this seemingly insignificant school? Well, from 1980-2010, their men's swim team won 31 consecutive NCAA national championships! On top of that, from 1984-2000, their women's swim team won 17 consecutive NCAA championships. Jim Steen was the coach for both the men's and women's swim teams during that time.

If there was ever a person who knew how to reload and keep the highest level of focus and dedication, Jim Steen is it. I cannot even imagine how difficult of a task it must have been to stay driven year after year. It almost begs the question, *"Does winning ever got old?"* When winning is the norm, it becomes much more challenging to keep yourself motivated.

It is not easy and it is a grind. Most competitors will never get the opportunity to lift a championship trophy above their heads even once. Perennial powerhouses are far and few between, so if you want to be a part of one, you better get ready to work harder than you ever imagined.

If you are fortunate enough to have more years of competing left, along with a team around you and a coach who knows what he or she is doing, do not miss the opportunity. Anything great worth *attaining* comes at a cost. Anything great worth *maintaining* costs even more. Are you willing to pay the price?

WHAT OTHERS SAY ABOUT *MAINTAINING*

"Winning takes talent, but to repeat takes character."
—John Wooden

"The higher a person climbs, the more his rear is exposed."
—Unknown

"Every successful person in the world is a hustler in one way or another. We all hustle to get where we need to be. Only a fool would sit around and wait on another man to feed him."
—K'wan

"It is very easy to come up with an excuse for why things will not happen in life, but champions accept that there are many things they cannot control, and instead, they master what they can." —David Becker

"Greatness only comes before hustle in the dictionary."
—Ross Simmonds

"Work like there is someone working 24 hours a day to take it away from you." —Mark Cuban

"Do not limit your challenges. Challenge your limits."
—Unknown

"Every champion was once a contender that did not give up."
—Gabby Douglas

"The question is not who is going to let me; it is who is going to stop me." —Ayn Rand

"You learn to always reach for the best in life and not settle for less; to stand out from the crowd and not except mediocrity. You will become a champion." —Mike Murdock

"With consistency and reps and routine, you are going to achieve your goals and get where you want to be."
—Mandy Rose

"Success is achieved and maintained by those who try and keep trying." —W. Clement Stone

"Consistency is the last refuge of the unimaginable."
—Oscar Wilde

"If today you are a little bit better than you were yesterday, then that is enough." —David A. Bednar

"You cannot be a winner without maturity and consistency."
—Marco Silva

"The best revenge is massive success." —Frank Sinatra

"Quitters never win. Winners never quit!" —Vince Lombardi

"The average is only consumed with today, but the champion is obsessed with tomorrow before it arrives; therefore, he or she plans for it." —Alex K. Mum

"There is the flash in the pan—the sudden success. But continued success is dependent upon tremendous attention to detail."
—Frederick Lenz

"When you look at people who are successful, you will find that they are the people who are motivated, but have consistency in their motivation." —Arsène Wenger

"Success is a lousy teacher. It seduces smart people into thinking they cannot lose." —Bill Gates

"Champions do not become champions when they win the event, but in the hours, weeks, months, and years they spend preparing for it. The victorious performance itself is merely a demonstration of their championship character." —Alan Armstrong

"It is not all about talent. It is about dependability, consistency, and being able to improve. If you work hard and you are coachable, and you understand what you need to do, you can improve." —Bill Belichick

"To be a champion, compete; to be a great champion, compete with the best; to be the greatest champion, compete with yourself." —Matshona Dhliwayo

"Success is never owned; it is rented—and rent is due every day." —Rory Vaden

"May my haters live very long to see my continued success, and to make their lives miserable." —Ziad Abdelnour

"Success is not final and failure is not fatal; it is the courage to continue that counts." —Winston Churchill

I/WE NEED TO BE BETTER AT _____ THAN LAST SEASON

1. _____

2. _____

3. _____

4. _____

5. _____

MAINTAINING PEAK LEVEL PERFORMANCE TAKES:

1. _____

2. _____

3. _____

4. _____

5. _____

Notes

Chapter 17

PERSEVERANCE

Carrying on in the face of adversity, pain, setback, or failure is very difficult. Nobody looks forward to any of these things. Despite this, athletes are always being forced to persevere in some way, shape, or form. Whether it is pushing yourself through the rigors of training and practice, battling through a hard-fought competition, or gutting it out through rehab and recovery—just so you can keep competing—you must have *perseverance*.

As I mentioned in the Attitude chapter, you cannot control what happens to you, but you can control how you respond. If there is one thing that stands out about people who keep a positive attitude—it is that they always find a way to persevere. Rain or shine, loss or victory, hurting or healthy...they just keep going.

We discussed strategies for looking ahead to potential adverse scenarios and how you should respond in the What If? chapter. Even if you know how you are *supposed* to respond, it does not suddenly make it easier to "walk the walk." How do you *actually* do it?

The truth is, perseverance comes down to toughness. More specifically—*mental* toughness. You may think you know what "tough" looks like, but there is no prototype. Toughness comes in all shapes and sizes. You do not need to be muscular, tall, or domineering to be tough. True toughness comes from within. It cannot be observed simply by looking at someone.

For example, I witnessed Kerri Strug—a 105 lb gymnast—severely hurt her ankle during her first vault attempt in the 1996 Olympics.

She toughed it out and landed her second attempt, but broke her ankle in the process. That second vault earned Kerri an Olympic gold medal. She persevered through the pain and pressure of the situation, and achieved her dream.

Here is a different example of toughness: with about two minutes remaining in the 3rd quarter of Super Bowl 51, the New England Patriots were down 25 points to the Atlanta Falcons. Instead of throwing in the towel, Tom Brady and the Patriots made the greatest comeback in Super Bowl history.

Despite only scoring 3 points in the first 43 minutes of play (and giving up 28 points), the Patriots scored 31 points (and gave up 0 points) in the final 17 minutes. That took more mental toughness than physical toughness.

There are endless examples of teams and individuals persevering and overcoming because they never gave up. My point is, do not ever doubt that you can *persevere* in the face of difficulty. In most cases, you will end up exhibiting toughness, resolve, and focus that you did not even realize you were capable of.

If it is still *possible* for you to win, but you *choose* to give up because it will be difficult, that is a *decision* you have to live with. If you give your best effort and still end up losing, you should be able to walk away knowing you gave it your all. Losing sucks. But, there may be times that it is just not your day. Persevering after a loss builds character.

Even when it comes to your training, perseverance is about digging deep inside of yourself and never letting that defeatist voice win. There is always going to be a reason to sleep in, go half-speed, or call it quits. We covered this in the Self-Discipline chapter.

A lot of teams will adopt the focus phrase of "finish strong," because even if you run the full race, but stop one foot short of the finish line, you get nothing. Many are not willing to push themselves that little extra. All of the greatest competitors exhibit discipline with this. They always give one more rep in the weight room. One more sprint. One more "nothing but net" free-throw. One more flawless run-through before practice can be done. This is what it takes.

Whatever effort you do not make, whatever reps you do not do, whatever days you take off, you will NEVER get them back. Do you want to risk falling short of your goals because you were not willing to push yourself hard enough? What are you doing to be better than your opponents? More importantly, what are you doing today to make yourself better than you were yesterday?

I love this quote so much that it deserves to stand out from the others at the end of the chapter. Ernest Hemingway once said, *"There is nothing noble in being superior to your fellow man. True nobility is being superior to your former self."* If you are not trying to better yourself in some way each and every day, what are you doing?

Remember that perseverance is about choosing to push through when things do not go the way you want. If you experience setbacks, that is OK. Just make the choice to *persevere*. You can learn from the mistakes that were made and get better. The opposite of persevering is surrendering...which one is for you?

It is true: sports and life are not always filled with victories and celebrations. But it is the difficult times that make the good times feel so amazing. If you did not have to study to be eligible, push your body to its limits to earn victories, or push your mind to handle the pain and stress, it would not be as rewarding.

The human will is an incredible thing. History is made when people do extraordinary things in extraordinary situations. At the end of the day, you need to determine if you have the *will* to fight through whatever life and competition throw at you.

WHAT OTHERS SAY ABOUT *PERSEVERANCE*

"Do not judge me by my success, judge me by how many times I fell down and got back up again." —Nelson Mandela

"Out of suffering have emerged the strongest souls; the most massive characters are seared with scars." —Khalil Gibran

"We will either find a way, or make one." —Anibal Barca

"That which does not kill us, makes us stronger."
—Friedrich Nietzsche

"And one has to understand that braveness is not the absence of fear, but rather the strength to keep going forward despite the fear." —Paulo Coelho

"No matter how much falls on us, we keep plowing ahead. That is the only way to keep the roads clear." —Greg Kincaid

"Life is not easy for any of us. But what of that? We must have perseverance and, above all, confidence in ourselves. We must believe we are gifted for something and that this thing must be attained." —Marie Curie

"I can be changed by what happens to me. But I refuse to be reduced by it." —Maya Angelou

17: PERSEVERANCE

"We do not have to become heroes overnight. Just a step at a time, meeting each thing that comes up, seeing it is not as dreadful as it appeared, discovering we have the strength to stare it down." —Eleanor Roosevelt

"A hero is an ordinary individual who finds the strength to persevere and endure, in spite of overwhelming obstacles."
—Christopher Reeve

"Character cannot be developed in ease and quiet. Only through experience of trial and suffering can the soul be strengthened, ambition inspired, and success achieved."
—Helen Keller

"Difficulties are meant to rouse, not discourage. The human spirit will grow strong with conflict." —William Ellery Channing

"Strength does not come from winning. Your struggles develop your strengths. When you go through hardships and decide not to surrender, that his strength." —Arnold Schwarzenegger

"The world breaks everyone and afterward, some are strong at the broken places." —Ernest Hemingway

"Make up your mind that no matter what comes your way, no matter how difficult, no matter how unfair, you will do more than simply survive. You will thrive in spite of it." —Joel Osteen

"With ordinary talent and extraordinary perseverance, all things are attainable." —Thomas Foxwell Burton

"Persistence can change failure into extraordinary achievement."
—Mark Levy

"The difference between the impossible and the possible lies in a person's determination." —Tommy Lasorda

"The more difficult the victory, the greater the happiness in winning." —Pele

"Obstacles do not have to stop you. If you run into a wall, do not turn around and give up. Figure out how to climb it, go through it, or work around it." —Michael Jordan

"A champion is someone who gets up, even though he does not want to." —Jack Dempsey

"It is hard to beat a person who never gives up." —Babe Ruth

"Winners never quit and quitters never win." —Vince Lombardi

"I have not failed. I have just found 10,000 ways that will not work." —Thomas Edison

"You build on failure. You use it as a steppingstone. Close the door on the past. You do not try to forget the mistakes, but you do not dwell on it. You do not let it have any of your energy, or any of your time, or any of your space." —Johnny Cash

"Many of life's failures are people who did not realize how close they were to success when they gave up." —Thomas Edison

"Only those who dare to fail greatly can ever achieve greatly."
—Robert F. Kennedy

TIMES I PERSEVERED AND DID NOT GIVE UP:

1.

2.

3.

4.

5.

TIMES I GAVE UP AND NOW REGRET:

1.

2.

3.

4.

5.

Notes

Chapter 18

MENTAL HEALTH

Note: Some readers will not need a lot of what is contained in this chapter. However, the subject of mental health is largely under-addressed and taboo to talk about—in athletics and beyond. So, even if there is only one person who benefits from what is contained here, I will consider it absolutely necessary for its inclusion in this book.

As competitors, we are conditioned to be physically and mentally tough. We handle whatever is thrown at us. We are warriors. We do not show weakness—we push through. We do not take the day off—we show up and put in work. We do not let our teammates, coaches, family, or friends down—there are too many people counting on us.

When we first get into athletics, we do it for the love of the game and we could never imagine getting to a point where sports are contributing to our stress or our unhappiness. We may not even realize how or when it happens, but suddenly, the joy is no longer there.

Years of enjoying sports can make us deny or intentionally ignore the fact that competing is not fun anymore. Even when we know it might be time to walk away, it is extremely hard to go down that road. Because of this, it can be very difficult for us to take a step back and acknowledge that we are not OK.

Mental health problems are pervasive in the United States and around the world. There does not seem to be enough support or openness for people to have conversations about their mental health struggles, either. Sometimes the struggles are brief and sometimes they can go on for years. Either way, we all need help processing things sometimes—and there is nothing wrong with that. Let me repeat that: there is NOTHING wrong with needing help sometimes!

This chapter is meant to help you have an awareness for your mental health status and why it is good to ask for help when you need it. As much as I want to help you become the best competitor you can be, it is a higher priority for you to be the best version of *yourself*—even if that means walking away from athletics. At the end of the day, sports are insignificant compared to your mental health and overall well-being.

It is no secret that athletes have extra obligations that normal students do not have to worry about. Not only do you have to keep your grades up to stay eligible, you have to study your playbook, attend practices, lift/train, compete for a starting position, compete in games, and many other responsibilities that are demanded of you. It is consuming! This is no easy feat.

I am sure you agree it is difficult enough to handle the regular academic and social expectations of simply being a young adult—let alone the expectations of being a student-athlete. It is impressive how much you handle on a daily basis! Do not ever forget that there are people who are willing to help you keep up with everything on your plate. You just have to be willing to ask for help. If, for any reason, you happen to reach out for help and that person tells you to, "suck it up," or does not take you seriously, PLEASE ask someone else. Talk to someone who is more concerned about you as a person, as opposed to you as an athlete.

Another source of stress for some student-athletes is when they feel a responsibility to play sports for a reason other than that they enjoy it and want to do it. It becomes a burden if it is no longer about what the athlete wants to do (if given a choice). It becomes something the athlete does for the benefit of others.

Sometimes a parent will force their kid to play the same sport(s) they did, or a sport they never got the opportunity to play. Other times, the parent may be trying to re-live their glory days or trying to achieve the success they wish they had had when they were younger. All of these are examples of the parents trying to live *vicariously* through their son or daughter.

A lot of times it backfires because you cannot force someone to be passionate about something if they do not love it to begin with. That is not how it works. The only thing that should matter is what the athlete wants.

Mental stress can also occur when athletes want to provide for their families and they believe playing a sport is their only shot at doing that. There is nothing wrong with wanting to help the ones who helped you. It is honorable and respectable if you have the opportunity to help others by doing something you love.

However, sometimes when you take something that you do out of love, and turn it into something you do out of obligation...the enjoyment can go away. When this happens, the burden of guilt comes in. The athlete believes he or she will be letting their family down if they want to stop playing. Whether or not the family is actually putting guilt on the athlete is irrelevant; the guilt still exists and that burden can be hard to carry. You are not a meal ticket!

During one particular team meeting my freshman year at Ohio State, Coach Tressel said, *"The day will come when the cheering will stop for everyone in this room. When that day comes, you will need to figure out what it is you are going to do with the rest of your life."* This struck me on a profound level because I had never thought of it before.

My athletic career ended abruptly and my life was changed in a split second when I broke my neck. Not only was I stripped of being able to play the game I love, I was no longer able to do most of the things I love. It took me time to process through things, but I eventually learned that I am a lot more than just an athlete.

For any athlete, leaving sports (for any reason) is a really difficult thing to do. It is a major part of who we are. So, to leave behind something that we have identified with for years—something that we have poured our souls into—it can be very taxing on our mental health.

This chapter may not be helpful for most readers at this time, but this topic is important for everyone to be aware of. When the day comes for you to put organized sports in your rearview mirror, you should really discuss things with those you trust—parents/family, teammates/friends, coaches, sports psychologists, pastor, etc.

Whatever reason you have for deciding to walk away from sports is irrelevant, really. Just be honest and open about how you feel. The truth is what is most important. Whether it is a choice, an injury, or if your goal of competing at the next level does not pan out—saying goodbye to athletics is never easy.

Just take things one day at a time and remember that you still have a lot to offer and you can still do incredible things outside the arena of athletics. Heck, you can even coach or be involved with sports in other ways. Pay it forward and help the next generation of athletes! Please remember there are plenty of options that will allow you to live a productive and happy life, long after your athletic career ends.

WHAT OTHERS SAY ABOUT *MENTAL HEALTH*

"Your mental health is everything—prioritize it. Make the time like your life depends on it, because it does." —Mel Robbins

"Sometimes when you are in a dark place, you think you have been buried, but you have actually been planted."
—Christine Caine

"When written in Chinese, the word 'crisis' is composed of two characters: one represents danger in the other represents opportunity." —John F Kennedy

"Keep your face always towards the sunshine—and shadows will fall behind you." —Walt Whitman

"We delight in the beauty of the butterfly, but rarely acknowledge the changes it has gone through to achieve that beauty." —Maya Angelou

"Getting over a painful experience is much like crossing the monkey bars. You have to let go at some point in order to move forward." —C.S. Lewis

"You do not need to see the whole staircase, just take the first step." —Martin Luther King Jr.

"I choose to make the rest of my life the best of my life."
—Louise Hay

"Everyone thinks of changing the world, but no one thinks of changing himself." —Leo Tolstoy

"I am only one, but I am one. I cannot do everything, but I can do something. And what I can do, I ought to do; and what I ought to do, by the grace of God, I shall do!"
—Edward Everett Hale

"Nothing can dim the light that shines from within."
—Maya Angelou

"You cannot go back and change the beginning, but you can start where you are and change the ending." —C.S. Lewis

"Only do what your heart tells you." —Princess Diana

"Learn to light a candle in the darkest moments of someone's life. Be the light that helps others see; it is what gives life its deepest significance." —Roy T. Bennett

"The struggle you're in today is developing the strength you'll need for tomorrow." —Robert Tew

"Change is the law of life. And those who look only to the past or present, are certain to miss the future." —John F. Kennedy

"There is hope, even when your brain tells you there isn't."
—John Green

"The secret of change is to focus all your energy, I am not on fighting the old, but I am building the new." —Socrates

"Nothing is stronger than a broken man rebuilding himself."
—Unknown

"Mental health is not a destination, but a process. It is about how you drive, not where you are going." —Noam Shpancer

"It is only when we take chances that our lives improve. The initial and most difficult risk that we need to take is to become honest." —Walter Anderson

"The adventure of life is to learn. The purpose of life is to grow. The nature of life is to change. The challenge of life is to overcome. The essence of life is to care. The opportunity of life is to serve. The secret of life is to dare. The spice of life is to befriend. The beauty of life is to give." —William Arthur Ward

"It is never too late for a new beginning in your life." —Joyce Meyers

"Change is painful, but nothing is as painful as staying stuck somewhere you do not want to be." —Mandy Hale

"Those who cannot change their minds cannot change anything."
—George Bernard Shaw

"Life is like riding a bicycle. To keep your balance, you must keep moving forward." —Albert Einstein

"When thinking about life, remember this: no amount of guilt can change the past and no amount of anxiety can change the future." —Umar Ibn Al-Khattaab

"Very little is needed to make a happy life; it is all within yourself, in your way of thinking." —Marcus Aurelius

IF I AM STRUGGLING MENTALLY, I KNOW I CAN TURN TO:

1. _____

2. _____

3. _____

4. _____

5. _____

MY MENTAL HEALTH IS IMPORTANT BECAUSE:

1. _____

2. _____

3. _____

4. _____

5. _____

Notes

Chapter 19

BEYOND THE GAME

In the very beginning of Chapter 1, I said being elite has little to do with your physical attributes. Having a stellar mentality is what is going to elevate you above your competition in sports. This is just as true when it comes to your endeavors *beyond the game.* Your athletic abilities are not going to save you if you cannot show up on time, cooperate with others, meet deadlines, focus, communicate, or be dependable.

One of the greatest things about sports is that they teach us a lot of important lessons that we will draw upon throughout our lives. Things like teamwork, resiliency, handling adversity, time management, commitment, and so much more. All the things I just mentioned can make you a better student, coworker, boss, spouse, parent, and person. Whether you are still competing in sports or your playing days are behind you, be sure to reflect on these lessons because they are so valuable.

Every chapter in this book can be applied to any area of life beyond the game. If you think about it, sports are just a metaphor for life. We work hard (as a team and independently) to push through challenges, conquer obstacles, accomplish our *goals*, and earn accolades. The mentality skills and traits you develop as an athlete will stick with you long after you step off the playing field...use your *strengths* to your advantage and lean on others if you need help with any *deficits*!

Your work ethic in sports should translate to your everyday life. Develop an effective *routine* that keeps you organized and efficient. Avoid *distractions* that will lead you down the wrong path. Maintain *self-discipline* that keeps you from becoming lazy and drifting through life without direction. Keep setting goals and striving for greatness, no matter what you choose to do beyond athletics.

Throughout your lifetime, you will be in situations where external circumstances are out of your control. The happiest and most successful people understand that when adversity hits them in the face, the most important thing they can control is their *attitude*. Nobody enjoys going through hard times, but the best way to change your circumstances is to maintain a positive attitude.

In the same way you need to keep your *composure* when you are in the middle of a game, match, or race that is not going your way, you need to think your way through situations that are not ideal at school, work, home or anywhere else. As I said before, we all get emotional and lose our cool at times. However, if you can improve your ability to stay calm in stressful situations, you will almost always come out ahead of those who cannot.

Effective *communication* skills are going to help you in pretty much any scenario you can think of. If you have not realized it already, you have to navigate through many dynamic situations and relationships. Negotiating, accommodating, and compromising are all part of communicating. Working together with your coach and teammates is very similar to cooperating with your teacher and classmates in school, boss and coworkers at your job, and your parents, siblings, roommates, etc. at home. You may not always agree or see eye to eye, but the best resolutions come by communicating.

Wherever you find yourself, do your best to be in a position of *leadership*, so you can impact others in a positive way. Even if you are not the boss or in charge, you should make it your *responsibility* to be a part of efforts to help others. Whether it is through volunteering for charities, organizing a community cleanup, or being a positive mentor or role model for the generation coming up, you should be the change you want to see in the world.

I know you want to be remembered as an incredible competitor, but you should be even more concerned about the legacy you leave behind as a person. When your time in this world is up and people reflect on the kind of person you were, what do you want them to say about you? You have the power to choose how you are remembered, based on the choices you make.

Everyone is capable of mastering everything contained in this book. Greatness, in some form, exists within every single person. When life gets hard (and it will), you cannot allow doubt, fear, or self-pity take over your *mentality*. Loss and failure are only the end of the road if you choose to give up or refuse to learn from it. Embrace it and improve from it—*perseverance* is the key!

I talked to you about *belief* in the beginning of the book because it is the foundation of having *confidence* and maintaining a winning mentality. You have the majority of your life ahead of you and it will be full of ups and downs. As long as you keep believing in yourself, you will always be on the road to success.

WHAT OTHERS SAY ABOUT *BEYOND THE GAME*

"Do anything, but let it produce joy." —Walt Whitman

"Happiness is a choice, a repetitive one."
—Akilnathan Logeswaran

"Greatness comes from fear. Fear can either shut us down and we can go home, or we can fight through it." —Lionel Richie

"The secret of life is enjoying the passage of time."
—James Taylor

"What lies behind us and what lies ahead of us are tiny matters compared to what lies within us." —Henry David Thoreau

"Participate in life instead of just watching it pass you by."
—Lindsey Wonderson

"Enjoy the little things in life, for one day you may look back and realize they were the big things." —Robert Breault

"Life is a game, play it; life is a challenge, meet it; life is an opportunity, capture it." —Unknown

"The saddest summary of a life contains three descriptions: could have, might have, and should have." —Louis E. Boone

"There will be two dates on your tombstone and all your friends will read 'em, but all that's gonna matter is that little dash between 'em." —Kevin Welch

"20 years from now you will be more disappointed by the things you didn't do, than by the things you did."
—Mark Twain

"Be bold and mighty forces will come to your aid. In the past, whenever I had fallen short in almost any undertaking, it was seldom because I had tried and failed. It was because I had let fear of failure stop me from trying at all." —Arthur Gordon

"One way to get the most out of life is to look upon it as an adventure." —William Feather

"Every day, it is important to ask and answer these questions: 'what's good in my life?' and 'what needs to be done?'"
—Nathaniel Branden

"A life without cause is a life without effect." —Barbarella

"Life has no limitations, except the ones you make." —Les Brown

"Life is a great big canvas and you should throw all the paint on it you can." —Danny Kaye

"Don't be afraid your life will end; be afraid that it will never begin." —Grace Hansen

"You only live once, but if you do it right, once is enough."
—Joe Lewis

"You were designed for accomplishment, engineered for success, and endowed with the seeds of greatness."
—Zig Ziglar

"Just do what must be done. This may not be happiness, but it is greatness." —George Bernard Shaw

"Few will have the greatness to bend history itself, but each of us can work to change a small portion of events, and in the total of all those acts, will be written in the history of this generation." —Robert Kennedy

"Whoever renders service to many, puts himself in line for greatness—great wealth, great return, great satisfaction, great reputation, and great joy." —Jim Rohn

"Everyone has their own greatness. Whether you reach your own greatness depends on your environment, your structure, the company you keep, and your attitude." —Ed Reed

"Greatness comes by doing a few small and smart things each and every day. Comes from taking little steps, consistently. Comes from making a few small chips against everything in your professional and personal life that is ordinary, so that a day eventually arrives, when all that is left is the extraordinary." —Robin S. Sharma

THE MOST IMPORTANT THINGS I LEARNED FROM THIS BOOK:

1. _____

2. _____

3. _____

4. _____

5. _____

THE MAIN THINGS I WILL WORK ON AFTER READING THIS BOOK:

1. _____

2. _____

3. _____

4. _____

5. _____

Notes

ABOUT THE AUTHOR

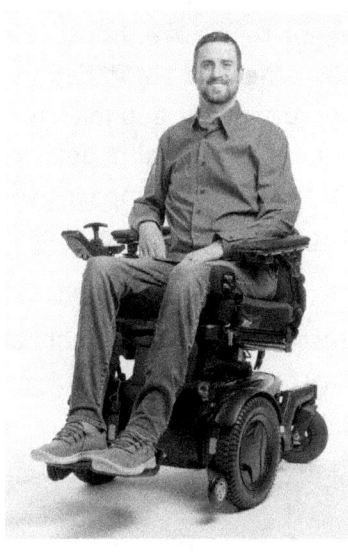

Tyson was born and raised in Ohio, where his passion for sports ignited at a young age. Excelling in football, basketball, and track, he achieved All-Ohio honors in track and etched his name in the record books as the leading receiver in his high school's history. His talent and drive allowed him to be recruited as a preferred walk-on at Ohio State, fulfilling a childhood dream.

During a team scrimmage in Tyson's sophomore year, a routine tackle resulted in a C4 spinal cord injury, paralyzing him from the neck down—a moment that would forever change his life. The road to recovery was long and challenging, involving two major surgeries to fuse his C3–C5 vertebrae and 2.5 months of intensive inpatient therapy. By the grace of God, Tyson was able to regain the use of his biceps. Despite the physical limitations and the challenges he has faced, his faith continues to grow and he is thankful for all the good that has come from his injury.

Tyson went on to graduate from Ohio State in 2009 with a bachelor's degree in Speech and Hearing Science, furthering his education with a Master's degree in Rehabilitation Counseling from the University at Buffalo. His personal experience ignited a desire to help others facing similar challenges, leading to the creation of New Perspective Foundation in 2014. This nonprofit organization has since provided nearly $500,000 to assist families affected by spinal cord injuries, helping them be present to support their loved ones during their recovery at the hospital.

Today, as a motivational speaker, Tyson inspires audiences across the nation, sharing his remarkable story of resilience, hope, and mental fortitude. His message encourages others to embrace life's adversities as opportunities for growth, self-discovery, and making a meaningful difference in the world. With unbreakable faith, determination and a heart full of gratitude, Tyson continues to impact lives, teaching others never to take anything for granted and to seize each day as a new chance to inspire change.

For more information or if you are interested in having Tyson speak to your group, please visit www.tysongentry.com.

www.ingramcontent.com/pod-product-compliance
Lightning Source LLC
LaVergne TN
LVHW051835080426
835512LV00018B/2883